How to Enjoy Your Retirement

How to Enjoy Your Retirement

John Sunshine

ama com A division of
American Management Associations

Library of Congress Cataloging in Publication Data

Sunshine, John.
    How to enjoy your retirement.

    Bibliography: p.
      1. Retirement.   2.   Men.   I.   Title.
HQ1062.S85   1975   301.43'5   74-78206
ISBN 0-8144-5367-8

Second Printing

Preface

IN MY six years of retirement I have talked with many retired men, and while working on the manuscript for this book I observed and interviewed countless others. Some are enjoying their new life style; others seem to be bored or restless.

Extra leisure can create problems, particularly for those who are not used to it. In this book I offer practical, workable ways to help solve these problems. There are many things that retirees can do to keep in good shape mentally and physically—so many ways, in fact, that this book just scratches the surface. I realize that some readers—those who have an illness or physical handicap—may not be able to try out all my suggestions, but I hope everyone will find at least a few ideas of value.

There are several subjects that retired people may

be interested in which are *not* covered in this book. One is medical advice. On this subject I refer the reader to books written by physicians. Better still is a person's own doctor, who has the additional advantage of knowing what is best for each individual patient. Sex—which is, after all, a private, intimate experience between two people—is not discussed. Those who have sexual problems should consult a medical doctor, a psychologist, or a psychiatrist. Finally, financial and legal matters are not discussed, although some pointers, and occasional warnings where appropriate, are given.

AN APOLOGY TO WOMEN

In this book I have addressed myself almost entirely to men, although I know that many women also face retirement, and that in the future there will be many, many more. But whether fairly or unfairly, I have not attempted to include them mainly for one reason: I believe that women can adjust to retirement much more easily than men.

Women of my generation are accustomed to taking care of themselves at home, for by and large that has been their natural habitat. A man who tries to take care of himself at home alone makes a mess of the job. Women make friends more readily than men, women adapt to change more easily, and on the whole women are better in a crisis. Except for financial reasons, I have not heard any woman say, "How will I manage without my husband?" On the other hand, most widowers are like lost dogs.

The wives of most men aged 65 and over tend to be younger and healthier than their husbands. More often than not, they are active women who may have difficulty in adjusting to their husband's retirement if he becomes dependent on them for companionship. And so it is the men who need help. They need to be self-reliant in keeping busy, alert, and physically fit, and if this book can help my readers accomplish that, then women will profit from it at least indirectly.

Retirement is what you make it: It can be dull or it can be a lively adventure. It all depends on whether you take advantage of the opportunities available to you—and I hope that in this book I've given some idea of how numerous those opportunities really are.

JOHN SUNSHINE

Contents

How to Enjoy
Your Retirement

Retirement: Danger or Opportunity?

THE Chinese use symbols instead of words. For the word *crisis,* they use two symbols—one means *danger* and the other means *opportunity*.

There is no doubt that retirement is a crisis. It offers those who retire a life of danger or opportunity.

The only people ideally suited for retirement are little children. They can always find something to do, and they have the energy to do it. They have imagination and curiosity, two keys that unlock a world of interests. They acquire friends quickly and easily no matter where they are, and they find so many things of mutual interest to discuss that they are never at a loss. They can adjust to any kind of weather and enjoy it. A lost dog is smart enough to team up with them. He knows he will have a marvelous time, that he will get their attention and kindness, and perhaps find a home.

There are mature people who, like little children, can find relaxation or pleasurable activity in almost anything. Others can readily resign themselves, permanently, to anything—retirement or even prison. I continue to wonder whether or not they are fortunate in being able to do so.

But let's face it: Although we may have been expert and very successful in our jobs, not many of us had the time, the energy, or even the opportunity to prepare ourselves to tackle other jobs with the same ability and intelligence. That's why corporations have different men for different jobs: presidents, advertising managers, sales managers, production managers, mechanics, right down the line.

Retirement is a new kind of job, one that requires adjustments as any other new job does, no matter how much experience you had in your own field. You probably had a certain amount of choice in your career, but on this occasion you have no choice. You must accept this new job. And that means that you will have to adjust to it—or lose the wonderful opportunity retirement offers.

In the six years of my retirement I have carefully observed many other retired men, and I have taken every opportunity to engage in conversation with them. A number of them told me of the mistakes they made, some of which were surprisingly similar to those I made. More surprising was my realization that too many were not doing anything to correct those mistakes, because they were completely resigned to continue to drift with the tide. That's a self-defeating attitude, and most of these men had no better reason for doing that than laziness.

I have also had interviews with men who were approaching retirement. Many of them expressed a fear of that future. There were several who were past retirement age and who held onto their job or business out of that fear. Every one of them said it was because they were afraid they would not find anything to do when they retired.

The only people who make an easy success of retirement are hobos and playboys. They've been at it all their lives.

Two traps are waiting for a man who reaches 65 and is retired from his work. First, retirement comes at a time when, because of his advanced age, this man is least able to cope with change, and second, all of us, young as well as old, are set back by a too-sudden change.

Unless your company makes retirement at 65 mandatory, hold onto your job as long as you can. Yes, hold onto it, especially if you enjoy the work and the companionship of your fellow workers. You may experience occasional tensions on that job, but those tensions are familiar and you know how to cope with them. Retirement is a new job and it could be one with a lot more tension. Why rush into it?

In addition, with a job you're a surfboard and you can ride it on the wave of inflation and take your time reaching the shore of retirement. With prices what they are, and inflation what it is, you'll find that you can use those extra dollars later on.

If you are in a business of your own, hold onto that business as long as you can. If you still want to or must sell out, do everything possible to have the new takeover organization retain your services in some capacity. Doctors, lawyers, accountants, or people in certain other professions can continue their professional activities on a part-time basis.

Frankly, I don't feel sorry for myself or my fellowmen who also are retired. My sympathy goes to the boys and young men who are retired because of poor physical or mental health or because they have been disabled by war. We old men have lived a full, productive life, while those boys and those young men did not, and didn't even have the chance. I believe that everyone will agree with me on this, but since this is a dissertation on *our* kind of retirement, let's get back to it.

Retirement comes after you've been driving on a long, rather smooth highway, relaxed at the wheel most of the time. You reach retirement when that highway suddenly ends and a sign says: *Detour ahead—Proceed at your own risk.*

Yes, retirement can mean danger or opportunity, and it's very much up to you which it will be. Remember, the sign says *Detour.* It's not the end of the road. The sign also warns: *Proceed at your own risk.* Let's see what, if anything, can be done to reduce that risk.

ON MAKING DECISIONS

While you were working, it may often have been necessary to make decisions in a hurry, even under pressure. Now that you are retired, or facing retirement, do take a little more time to make decisions which you may have to live with for the rest of your life.

It is true that some problems solve themselves if

you leave them alone. If decisions *have* to be made, however, try to make them yourself. Do not allow the advice of friends or relatives to be too important a factor when decisions have to be made. A small problem can become a big problem if you get too much advice.

This is not to suggest that you be so stubborn that you become a prisoner of your own opinions. If a legal decision is involved, consult your lawyer. If it's a medical decision, consult your doctor. If it's a financial decision, be careful whom you consult.

No matter what you do, you will, at times, make the wrong decision. When you do, smile and forget it, for it may have prevented you from making a worse one. Everyone makes wrong decisions at times—even the amazing computers make mistakes.

Last, but not least, don't take everything too seriously. Sometimes when you realize you've made a bad decision you'll have enough time to correct it. And there are times when the wrong decision can turn out to be a lucky break—for you.

MONEY: THE IMPORTANCE OF SAYING NO

Here is one area where, unless you have unlimited retirement funds, you *can't* afford to make quick decisions and not worry about them. It is strange and unfortunate that too many people believe most retired men are well off financially, or that they no longer have any financial problems. The cost of living, for the vast majority of retired people, does not drop enough to make up for the difference between their former income and their retirement income, a condition that grows steadily more difficult under conditions of inflation.

Be careful in the use of your funds, for the chances of replacing money you give away are practically non-existent. The first use, and in most cases the only use, of those funds should be for the comforts you and your wife have earned. Take care of yourselves, for it is indeed sad if you end up depending on your children or anyone else. Your children will be thankful if you are able to provide for your wife and yourself and they do not have to.

The power of the word *no* was well illustrated when women refused to accept the midi style. Inability to say no can cost a great deal in comfort, health, time, and money. After you retire, it is more important than ever to be able to say no.

No matter how much money you give or lend to some people, especially relatives, it is never enough. It may even embitter them toward you, for they will always think you could well afford to have given *more*.

Too many of us gave our children the necessities of life without a struggle on their part, and now too many of them want the luxuries of life without a struggle. But when people are helped too much, more harm than good is done. Hats off to the young man who said to his father: "You're spoiling me with what you're doing for me; if you do too much more, you'll *ruin* me."

If you have enough money to enable you to live in reasonable comfort, and if you do all you possibly can to put aside a surplus for your children, grandchildren, or other relatives, that's your business and not mine. However, my advice is that you not make too many sacrifices to accomplish that generous and kind action. Make sure, at least, that your children, grandchildren, or other relatives are really concerned about your well-being and not just interested in the provisions of your will. They may not have the time to visit you now, but they surely will manage to be present when your lawyer is ready to read your will to them. (Incidentally, it is a good idea to review your will each year.)

Things that people get for nothing are unappreciated. Inherited money goes down the drain faster than any other money.

I am reminded of my retired lawyer's favorite story about an elderly couple who had been clients of his for many years. He always believed they were not well off financially, and he considered them below average in intelligence, but every year they spent many months traveling on rather expensive trips to all parts of the world. Just before he retired he asked them apologetically where they got the money to make all those expensive trips. When they told him that those trips were being paid for by their heirs, he changed his mind about their financial condition and their intelligence.

Under no circumstances should you extend a loan when there is even the slightest chance that it will not be repaid. Remember, you are retired and can no longer afford to lose money. If you have the wherewithal to make your retired life comfortable and enjoyable, you should manage your funds well enough to make that comfort and enjoyment possible.

Finally, a more general caution: Do not take on *any* obligation which you may have difficulty in fulfilling. Retired people should be extra careful about making promises. Promises can be foolish—even perilous. Circumstances beyond our control may prevent us from keeping them, and those waiting for promises to be kept may not understand—or may *refuse* to understand—the circumstances. It might be advisable to discharge financial and other obligations before retirement.

Remember, proper management requires the courage to say no. During your working life you may have found it *advisable* to turn people down. During retirement, the ability to turn people down is a downright *necessity*.

HOW TO LIVE LONGER

Some people live to a very old age no matter what they do, what they eat, or what they drink. Perhaps it's a matter of inheriting a strong constitution and just plain good chemistry. But whatever the explanation, you can be pretty sure that something they all have is a will to live, a cheerful attitude, and an active mind.

It may not seem so, but the first two qualities are byproducts of the third. Activity not only will make you live longer but will open the door to an interesting, enjoyable, longer life. It gives you a reason for living, and it gives you purpose and direction.

Recently I read of a study made by a leading life insurance company showing that scientists rank first among those who live to an advanced old age, then clergymen and educators. The report gave no reasons, but it is obvious that scientists and educators are forever students with busy minds, enjoying the search for answers to the problems that intrigue them. As for clergymen, they have great dedication and gain a lot of satisfaction from helping people.

There is no way of guaranteeing that your mind and body won't slow down as age increases, but here is a list of people, recognizable to everyone, who have continued to live active lives: Jack Benny, movie and television star (80 going on 40); Thomas Hart Benton, artist (85); James Bryant Conant, educator (81); Jack Dempsey, restaurateur (79); Jimmy Durante, whirlwind entertainer (81); Averell Harriman, diplomat (83); John S. Knight, newspaper editorial chairman (79); Alice Roosevelt Longworth, known to every politician as a fixture in Washington, D.C., society (90); George Meany, labor leader (80); Artur Rubinstein, pianist (85); Leopold Stokowski, orchestra conductor (92); Gloria Swanson, former movie star, now involved in health foods and fashion (75); Lowell Thomas, lecturer, traveler, author (82); Marshal Tito, President of Yugoslavia (82); Arnold J. Toynbee, historian (85); Mark Van Doren, educator, poet (80).

Others who have died in recent years are Pearl S. Buck, author (80); Pablo Casals, cellist, composer, and orchestra conductor (96); Sir Winston Churchill (91); Charles de Gaulle (80); Albert Einstein (76); Edward Everett Horton, actor (84); General Douglas MacArthur (84); Sol Hurok, impressario (85); J. C. Penney, industrialist (95); Pablo Picasso, painter and

sculptor (91); Grandma Moses (Anna Mary Robertson), artist (101); Vilhjalmur Stefansson, explorer
(83); Paul Dudley White, heart specialist (87).

These people were engaged in various fields, but
the important thing is that they led active, busy lives
right up to their last day.

Gerontologists agree that the mind does not dete-
riorate just because a person grows old, and our lists
certainly offer proof of that. As for the ability to be
physically active, it may *slow* down, but not necessarily *break* down.

The Soviet News Agency (Tass) reported that it
checked 81 persons over 100 years of age, living in a
small village in the foothills of the Caucasus Mountains, and found that they attributed their longevity
to hard work and eating honey. I agree on hard work.
As for honey, all I can say is that Socrates recommended eating it as an aid to a long life. He lived to
only 70, but who knows—he might have lived many
more years if he had not been forced to drink hemlock!

Japan's Health and Welfare Ministry recently
made a study of more than 1,000 persons of 90 years
and over, and reported that 99 percent of them were
talkative and sociable. You can't be talkative and
sociable without being active and meeting and mixing
with other people. The Ministry also reported that
nearly 75 percent preferred sweet food, so perhaps
there is some truth to the value of honey. In ancient
times, honey was considered a youth elixir.

In an entirely different part of the world—a
mountainous region of South America—there is a village where people live 10, 20, and more years beyond

the 100 mark, in good health and vigor. Articles about them have appeared in magazines and newspapers, and radio and television have reported on them.

They smoke a lot of homemade cigarettes and drink a lot of rum, but they lead a simple life, free of stress, and therefore free of a basic cause of heart disease. Although they are hard workers, they eat only one-third the amount of food we Americans eat. Since walking is their general means of transportation, their exercise is doubly healthful, because walking up and down hills not only stimulates circulation and tones up the entire body, it is also excellent for the heart, provided you are accustomed to it. (That is why climbing stairs regularly is good for you.)

There is still another factor that may help them. Because they live in a mountainous region, their drinking water undoubtedly contains minerals, which some specialists believe may be good for the heart.

Let's look into the life of one man who lived to be 99 and who wrote his prescription for a long life when he was 91. Luigi Cornaro was born in Venice, Italy, in 1467. A member of the nobility, he had the time and the money to indulge in a continuous round of parties, twice each day, at which food and wine were served in large quantities. By the age of about 45, he suffered continual stomach pains and attacks of fever and gout. His condition finally reached a stage where he realized that death would soon come to him, as it did to all his friends in their late forties.

He gave serious thought to his condition and determined to find the cause of it. He finally arrived at the conclusion that it must be due to the large quantities of food and wine he and the others consumed at those parties.

Cornaro then decided to discontinue all medicines and to make a drastic cut in the total amount of food he ate. He divided that much smaller amount into four, carefully weighed portions, which he consumed as four meals each day. He drank a small glass of wine at each of those four meals and said that wine is, indeed, the milk of old age.

His health and clearness of mind regained, he determined to make himself useful. He was a firm believer that not being active and not shouldering some responsibilities were detrimental for anyone, especially during old age.

As his condition continued to improve, he went for long walks, which he greatly enjoyed. He made it a point to meet and converse with men proficient in their fields so that he could learn something new. He added further interest to his life by reading and writing, and he became useful by volunteering his services to his city and country.

At 91 years of age, he wrote his famous book on how to obtain good health of mind and body and, in so doing, be able to enjoy life into ripe old age.

How to Live One Hundred Years, written more than 400 years ago, continues to be reprinted in many languages. The book is not in great demand by the general public, so bookstores don't stock it. If your library does not have a copy, you can obtain an excellent small, hardcover issue from Health Publishing Co., 2126 34th Avenue, San Francisco, California 94116. Your request should be accompanied by a check or money order for $2.75 plus 16 cents postage.

HOW TO LOOK YOUNGER, FEEL YOUNGER, BE YOUNGER

Why do women seem to age more slowly than men? Without trying to be scientific or profound, we can see a few special reasons right off the bat:

1. Women make a determined effort to stay younger-looking longer. Most women start looking 40 at about the time they reach 50.
2. Women dye their gray hair. No woman ever wants to think of herself as distinguished-looking.
3. Most women continue to wear younger-looking clothes.
4. They resorted to plastic surgery long before the men.
5. Watch a woman going into a beauty shop, and then watch her come out. She looks younger, feels younger, and with her smile and spry walk, *is* younger.

Women adapt to change—a vital, mind-activating thing. They even look for changes—a new hairdo, a different arrangement of furniture, a new way to prepare certain foods—and it works wonders. Boredom and routine are the worst enemies of the spirit of youth. In fact, boredom is the expressway on which we travel the fastest to old age. Mind you, we can be proud to achieve a long life of many years. (It's rather odd that although some young people frown on those who are old, they hope to get there themselves.) But it's an old spirit we never want to see. And so, in addition to keeping active and maintaining a good mental attitude, what else can you do to attain and keep that feeling of youth?

Celebrating birthdays is a mistake. Birthdays are special occasions, but keep the observances small. Festivities are fine for children, but a party for a man can overemphasize his age and take away from his esteem.

Don't deny your calendar age if you might later regret it. Even if you don't broadcast your age to your friends, always be honest about your age in legal matters or public records or statements.

Don't let your appearance slip. You don't have to look like a fashion advertisement, but your appearance will be greatly helped by clean, neatly pressed clothing that is appropriate and well put together in color scheme. Wearing a tie can make you feel dressed up. Modish clothes—if not too extreme—can certainly help your spirits and convey a sense of pride.

Then again, all you may need is a shave. A two-day growth of beard can make you feel shabby, and an accidental meeting with a friend will cause needless embarrassment.

If you plan an evening out, take a lesson from your wife's visits to the beauty salon. Go to your barber and have him give you the full treatment.

A young man may want to look older, so he wears a mustache or a beard. But that's not your problem—if you have either one, cut it off; if both, cut them off. Don't wear sideburns that are so ornamental they make you look like a character in an 1890 painting. If you don't want to dye your hair (it really isn't necessary), try wearing it a different way.

Smile. You've never heard anyone say "the old cheerful," but you have certainly heard "the old grouch." So start the day with a smile and let it grow. If you are cheerful in spirit and mentally young, you'll never have difficulty mixing with younger people.

Reduce your intake. We all enjoy eating, but if you want to live longer, don't eat too much at one meal. It makes good sense to eat smaller meals, perhaps more often, as Cornaro did.

A good way to eat less is to eat slowly. Put less food on your plate and take longer to finish it. That way you can fool your stomach and satisfy your conscience. Engaging in conversation with another person while eating is also an aid to eating more slowly. Perhaps one reason women outlive men by five or more years is that they eat less food in order to retain their figures.

Wise old Benjamin Franklin said, "To lengthen thy life, lessen thy meals."

Visit your doctor once a year for a thorough checkup. Just about every illness, if caught in time, can be cured, arrested, or controlled. In view of the great, rapid advances being made through medical research, each year that we can add to our life makes possible a bonus of one, or five, or ten, or even more years.

Take vacations. Vacations are good for everyone and provide a necessary change of pace and scenery, especially for the retired person. Several short vacations are often better than a single long one.

Have confidence and respect for yourself. Stand up and be counted. If you keep yourself active, cheerful, and interested, others will find you attractive and want you around them. Even young people will be attracted to you. A mixture of both young and older people—who are interesting—is psychologically healthful. It offers many advantages for the young, and exhilarates and rejuvenates older persons.

Finally, if you are a considerate and noble husband, you will not pay attention to any of my suggestions and will not concern yourself with trying to be younger than you are, for the older you look, *the younger your wife will look.*

GIVE YOURSELF
A BETTER-THAN-EVEN BREAK

The apartment or home some retired people furnish turns out to be beautiful, but not comfortable. It should not be necessary to impress people to the extent that your living quarters look like a window display. Even if you live an active life, you will be spending more time at home after you retire, and it should be comfortable.

Household help, like everything else, is expensive. And even if you can afford it, such help has become increasingly difficult to find. Therefore, plan your living quarters for easy maintenance.

Don't furnish with housekeeping features that pin you down. If you have possessions of such value that you worry about them, or if you can't leave because of animals or plants, your house becomes your prison.

Remember, your retirement upsets your wife's previous routine and means additional work for her. Encourage her to go into semi-retirement by making your home a place to be lived in, not looked at.

If you can afford it, try to have one little extra

room as a den. It will get you out of your wife's way and will serve as an "escape hatch" to give you a little privacy.

Have your own small desk for writing letters, paying bills, keeping files, and storing writing accessories. A desk can be a great comfort to someone who has spent most of his working life behind one and feels incomplete without it.

Deep-cushioned chairs and sofa are certainly attractive and comfortable, but if you plan to do a lot of sitting, be sure to have a plain, straight-backed chair on hand—it is much better for your back. Use a footrest to raise your legs a little if the backs of your thighs press against the seat. A folding chair can be folded and placed out of sight when visitors are coming if your wife objects to its appearance.

If you enjoy company, do try to see that the kitchen is a really large room, or at least open enough for people to feel free about wandering in and out. That way your guests can help with preparation and cleaning up, and conversation isn't lost to whoever is in the kitchen.

Most of us enjoy having a garden, but unless it's a hobby, how about letting things grow a little wild so that you can sit down and enjoy that garden instead of spending so much time taking care of it?

If you build a home in a warm-climate area, request a broad overhang on one side so that you can have an outdoor shaded, protected area. You'll be glad to get away from the hot sun, and rain won't prevent you from cooking on an outdoor grill. You can protect outdoor furniture or equipment without having to bring it inside.

A fireplace is a lovely thing to have. It gives us a sense of comfort and protection, especially as we grow older. There are some nights even in southern Florida when the warmth of an open fire is welcome and relaxing.

If you enjoy reading or engage in a hobby that requires good lighting, try to work near a window with northern exposure. Having a window in that location provides a steady light during most of the daylight hours.

If you live in a warm-climate area and have two or more bedrooms, be prepared for visiting relatives and friends when it's cold up North. Here are some recommended house rules, to be sent to those who plan to visit you:

- Please notify us of the exact date of your arrival and await our approval to be sure that *your* convenience suits *our* convenience.
- All visitors are respectfully but firmly requested to abstain from criticizing their host and hostess.
- There will be no charge for the room, linens, water, and electricity, but food costs are to be shared on an equal basis.
- Guests must help with household chores to the extent of tidying up the rooms they use and cleaning up their own spills.
- Parents will be financially responsible for damage done by their children.

You may have some others to add, or, if you can afford it, you may not expect guests to share in the cost of food. But the point is that you should be honest about letting your visitors know what you expect of them. That way you won't find yourself developing a grudge against someone for doing something that you are too embarrassed to bring out in the open.

MEETING THE CHALLENGE

The object of this book is to help you avoid certain risks and be prepared for others (or, where there is no choice, adjust to them). Since there are too many individual circumstances to permit general rules or suggestions, this book, at best, can serve only as a guide.

The final decisions must be made by you. Now, more than ever, *it is your life*. Perhaps, to be fair, all those directly involved in such decisions should be given consideration. But your greatest concern must be for yourself. Retirement can be a new life—and a great life—if you know what to do with it.

There's No Need to Be Lonely

LONELINESS is a hard thing to live with. During the years of activity and involvement with our jobs and our growing families, there wasn't much opportunity for solitude. Now, without a place to be every morning, without ongoing responsibilities and chores, there is more opportunity than we want. It takes quite a while for most of us retired people to adjust to that situation, and some never do.

I was a traveling salesman for 41 years. For most of those years, like all traveling salesmen, I was away from home and friends for months at a time. (There were no airplanes in those years, and a man could not easily get home for the weekend.) There was no chance to get lonely during the five working days of the week. On those days I was kept busy rushing around trying to get orders during the day and doing my paperwork in the evenings. I met a lot of people and had plenty of opportunity for conversation, but it was and had to be one subject—business. Those men I called on were busy, and it was a cardinal rule for salesmen to do their talking about what was essential—their products—and then get out.

Yes, those five working days went along smoothly and interestingly. However, it took me quite some time to learn how to adjust to the loneliness I felt on weekends.

I got tired of too much reading, television had not yet been invented, and I never stopped in one place long enough to make friends. I realized that the answer —or at least the way to begin—was to keep as busy on weekends as I was during the week.

From then on, I checked the newspaper of the city I was in to see if there was some special event going on there or at some other place nearby. I went to the chamber of commerce to learn if there was some interesting or unusual place or thing to see in the vicinity.

When in Omaha, I visited the famous Boys Town located only ten miles away. While in Phoenix, Arizona, I made it a point to visit the Grand Canyon over the weekend. In Seattle, I spent a weekend on Mount Rainier. In Durango, Colorado, I took a one-day round trip to Silverton on a narrow-gauge railroad. In Chicago, I spent many days in that city's interesting Museum of Science and Industry. Those activities certainly gave me an opportunity to meet many people—and, if nothing more, a chance for conversation on some subject besides the chemical products I was selling.

Being alone too much dehydrates the mind and

soul. The way to prevent this dehydration is to water your spirit with the companionship of others, strangers as well as friends. Build bridges, not walls, as Joseph Fort Newton advised.

William Endicott, a staff writer of the *Los Angeles Times,* wrote a feature story about Mrs. Jean Rosenstein, who threw out lines to build such a bridge.

. . . An 84-year-old widow, she was living alone in a tiny apartment here, wanting some human contact so strongly that she wrote a pathetic letter to the *Los Angeles Times* and enclosed $1 with the plea that someone use it to call her.

The story was sent to hundreds of newspapers across the continent by the Los Angeles Times-Washington Post News Service, triggering a public response the likes of which I had not seen in a 14-year newspaper career. Mrs. Rosenstein apparently was symbolic of a major national disease, and it was not hate, or fear, or greed, or jealousy or any of the other baser human emotions.

It was, simply, loneliness.

Letters, literally thousands of them, poured in from all over the United States and Canada. They came from old people—as might be expected—but also from children, college students, servicemen, young mothers, airline stewardesses, young bachelors, airline pilots, middle-aged women.

I am not suggesting that you do what Mrs. Rosenstein did. I hope you haven't let things get to such a state. The best way to make certain that you *never* get to that state is to keep your human contacts active.

The remainder of this chapter will discuss two important contacts—friends and grandchildren. But first I should mention that, while contact with another human being is usually the best antidote for loneliness, a pet can be a good companion too. We can talk to a pet, and perhaps it will, in its own way, understand. A dog is generally the first choice. It takes us out of the house and offers the chance to talk to others who are walking their dogs. A cat requires less attention and should be the choice for those who cannot, for some reason, give the attention a dog requires. A parakeet can also be fun.

MEETING PEOPLE

If your circle of acquaintances is very small, or if you have moved to a new location and know no one there, you can take the initiative in many ways. The first step is to meet and be with other people. If you're new in town, find out whether there is a club composed of former residents of your home city or state. If so, join it. The members' common interests can lead to enjoyable and interesting conversations and often to friendships. Shared interests explain why artists congregate in artists' colonies, why colleges have fraternities, why actors join the Friars Club, why businessmen seek an executives' club, and why a veteran joins the American Legion or other veterans' organization.

Trade association conventions, where delegates are often competitors, are stimulating and enjoyable because those attending have something in common to talk about and share. In fact, conventions are great for rejuvenating older people.

You can also meet people in public places like parks, libraries, museums, zoos, churches, and beaches. Some cities have open-air concerts and theatrical performances, and most small towns have public auctions and bazaars from time to time. Many communities hold fairs and exhibitions—such as flower shows, needle-work shows, and exhibits of paintings—for local residents whose amateur activities are worth showing. Even if you don't participate, you'll enjoy meeting the people who do. There is nothing like a shared interest to spark conversation and friendliness.

Joining adult education classes, whether the subject is intellectual, playing a musical instrument, or learning the art of bookbinding, is an obvious and stimulating way of finding people who share your interests. Classes are to be found in local colleges, in the local Y, and sometimes in private homes.

Travel, if you can afford it, provides an opportunity for meeting other travelers—who are likely to be cheerful and friendly, if only because they too are looking for the stimulation of new people and places. If you can't afford a real trip, even a short one, look into day excursions to special places of interest within the general vicinity of your town.

If you like to dance, you can easily find out where dances are held. If you don't know how, learn. Because dancing is so popular among older people, it's a wonderful way to meet others.

Many more suggestions—such as volunteer work and taking a job—are worthwhile not only for the interest and value of the work itself but also for the human contacts.

Talking with People

Both mental relaxation and mental stimulation can come through conversation with other people. We all need people to talk to, or have near us, and that is why bars and cocktail lounges are so popular. For better or worse, liquor does have a tendency to break down barriers between strangers.

The ability to talk interestingly is a magnet that attracts people to you and opens the door to friendship. Not everyone has the gift of gab—the ability to carry on an impersonal conversation and be entertaining— but the art of good talk can be cultivated. If it doesn't come easily to you, do some thinking about what it involves.

Close friends and family aside, ask yourself why you prefer to spend time with certain people instead of others. One thing that may come to mind is a person's disposition or attitude. We prefer to be with people who maintain and present a cheerful state of mind. Very few of us can *always* be cheerful, but if we want others to find our company pleasant, the least we can do is to make every effort to be pleasant when we are with them. Most people enjoy talking to others, whether they are lonely or not. Let us not repel them by wearing a lonely look.

Of course, cheerfulness is not the only thing that makes you seek out a person's company. If you think again about the people you like best, you'll find that they're the ones who stimulate you without angering or annoying you. They pique your interest with anecdotes about their experiences—travel, personalities, jobs—or they amuse you with jokes or funny things that have happened to them, or they excite your mind or imagination. It is interesting also to look at what these people do *not* do. They do not talk constantly about their problems, and in fact they often don't talk at all. Don't forget that conversation is a two-way street; we must give the other person a chance to do some talking also. It is good to remember that most of us would rather talk than listen, and we will not get other people to listen to us unless we are willing to listen to them.

I must admit, however, that it's hard to listen to people when they get onto certain topics—particularly their problems. In real life, things don't happen to people in quite such dramatic form as they do in the soap operas of radio and television. When those stories bore us we can switch them off. It's much harder to switch off someone who has launched on a long tale of woe.

In fact, next time you are tempted to talk about your own problems, remember the impatience you felt when last hearing someone else's. Except with old, close friends, it is advisable to avoid telling others about your troubles. It is boring, and the other person may have greater problems than yours.

If someone insists on telling you about his problems, though, it might be worth the patience to listen. Perhaps eventually the talk will shift to something else that is amusing or interesting. It is even possible that some people's problems will in themselves prove dramatic and arouse our interest. Also, remember that when other people talk about their personal lives, in a way they are asking for our understanding and sympathy. And we cannot expect others to extend true friendship to us if we do not extend it to them.

Conversation Topics

There are an infinite number of things to talk about. Naturally, you must try to gain some insight into what subjects interest the person you are with. But there are a few general rules that apply to everyone.

First, there are the topics that lead to bad feelings or arguments:

Politics. The only people who will listen to you are those who happen to agree with you. A good way to start an argument is to try to influence another person's vote or to sway his thinking about a political issue or official. Usually it's a waste of time to boot, because most people won't be swayed.

Religion. In this country, religion is strictly a personal matter, so leave it strictly alone.

Sports. If you and another person share an interest in a particular sport, the chances are you can't tell him anything he doesn't already know—and I have seen friends get into a bitter argument over the subject. On the other hand, such arguments rarely end in personal dislike, and some people get a kick out of them.

Second, there are the topics that bore other people and usually lead to a dead end:

The weather. As Mark Twain said, everybody talks about the weather. So be different and avoid the subject.

Your troubles. Don't talk about them. DON'T TALK ABOUT THEM. DON'T TALK ABOUT THEM.

Your grandchildren. I never met grandparents who didn't love to tell you all about them: their looks, their talents, their funny sayings, their school and sports accomplishments, anything that pleases them. The problem is that the only grandchildren people are really interested in is their own, so talk about yours with your spouse.

Now for some neutral areas:

The news. Most people read the newspapers and watch television, and they know what is going on as well as you do. But there is always something happening that warrants discussion, and many events are just so unusual that people wonder about them and like to cross-check their reactions.

The arts. Even if you live in a community where there is no theater or concert hall, there are books and movies available everywhere to everyone. Most people are interested in at least one aspect of the arts, and if you find someone who shares a special liking for your favorite author or film star, you'll find hours of pleasant conversation for both of you.

People are likely to have interesting things to say about any subject that they have taken the trouble to know something about. If you can be tactful about drawing people out, you'll be sure to find some area—whether it's gardening, collecting coins, or playing old tunes—that you both enjoy talking about.

Human interest stories. Newspapers and magazines are full of articles about people and places and discoveries. If you find something that especially interests you, chances are that it will interest others.

You will find plenty of current reading materials at your public library. The magazines of broadest general interest are *Newsweek, Reader's Digest, U.S. News & World Report,* and *Time.* Newspapers of national interest that are sufficiently important to be carried by local libraries include *The Christian Science Monitor, The National Observer, The New York Times,* and *The Wall Street Journal.*

Daily life. The small things that play a part of our everyday life are always good for small talk. Women seem to enjoy talking about household techniques and swapping recipes. Men, if they used to be in the same business or job, get a kick out of exchanging experiences.

Travel. If you have been to some especially interesting or unusual places, you will have interesting things to relate. But remember, self-interest is the deepest human trait; people don't really want to sit quietly and listen to *you* tell about *your* experiences. If you find someone who has been to the same place, you will both enjoy exchanging stories and impressions. But don't otherwise expect people to listen patiently to your tales.

People love to talk about their hometown. All I have to do to start a conversation is ask: "Where are you from?" Wherever I happen to be, I find that most people originally came from some other place. No matter how much they enjoy living where they are, they love to hear what others have to say about "home." Since I traveled extensively as a salesman, I have usually visited that town or at least been to one close enough to make it interesting. Without fail I get a pleasant response.

Finally, I suggest astrology as an unfailing topic. Almost everyone has some interest in it because it appeals to self-interest. *Time* magazine not too long ago devoted several pages to astrology as a subject of wide interest, and almost every newspaper features a daily horoscope. Ask people for their astrological sign and chances are that they will know it. Their eyes will light up waiting for you to say something about that sign, and their interest will intensify when you hit on even one of their character traits.

You can pick up little, inexpensive books on each astrological sign in the five-and-dime and other stores.

Don't bother with the fortune-telling part; concentrate on the points relating to character traits. Make notes of the major characteristics and memorize them, or carry the notes with you. Before long, you'll be an expert. At the very least, even the people who have no use for astrology will get a kick out of being told what the books say about them.

GOOD FRIENDS

This chapter has placed great emphasis on conversation—not just because conversation is pleasant in itself but because it can be the first step on the road to lasting friendship.

Retirement increases the need for friends—or at least, association with other people. You may not have made friends of the people who worked with you, but you did have many things in common to discuss with them. If you miss your job, it may be largely because you miss *them*.

One of the reasons we enjoy television is that it brings people into our home, even if the people are only pictures with motion and sound. If we want to go to bed early or do something else, we can tell them it's time to go home by simply turning off the set. But don't make the mistake of allowing television to be your only means of having people visit you. It should not be a continuous substitute for real-life friends.

Few pleasures give more satisfaction than talking with a friend. It can often create the magic of making time stand still. The best part of a fishing or hunting trip with old friends is the togetherness, not just the challenge of the sport or the joy that the outdoors affords.

Just sitting with a friend can be relaxing. A fine illustration of this was the friendship between Emerson and Thoreau. They had much in common and plenty to talk about, but occasionally they would spend several hours together without saying a word. When they parted, one or the other would comment on their pleasant visit. Such is the understanding warmth of friendship, for a friend does not ask for or need any explanation for what we do.

Daniel Defoe, the English author of *Robinson Crusoe,* was understanding enough to provide his hero with a companion, his man "Friday." They were together and not alone. The fact that they did not have a common language made little difference—they managed to communicate through gestures, and their cheerful willingness to help each other promoted an understanding that made for genuine and heartwarming companionship.

Although we do not need many friends, we do need several, because each has certain abilities, knowledge, or qualities we admire. These individual attributes are like the spreading branches of a tree, under which we can sit in enjoyment.

Unfortunately, making new friends becomes more difficult the older we get. It's not easy to replace comfortable and enjoyable old friends with new ones. Friendships need time to develop, and they grow riper and mellower with the passing years. New friends may be more exciting, but long-standing friendships are far more satisfying. If you are thinking of moving to a new location, give serious thought to old friends, your children, your grandchildren, and other relatives whom you may miss too much.

By the same token, you may want to move to a town where a number of good friends of yours are now living. But don't move to another location because you have a friend living there if it is someone you have not seen or communicated with for a long time. Remember that people change some of their ideas, habits, and interests as they grow older. You may think you can still enjoy each other, but that isn't always so. And it is also possible that you may not like that location or climate and become grouchy. As a result, you could lose that friend entirely.

Nor should you move somewhere just because you hear "The people are friendly there." That does not prevent unfriendly people from moving in! In fact, it may encourage them to do so in the hope that they may, at last, be able to make some friends.

Some people make friends anywhere, while others do not. I heard of a couple who moved from Cleveland to Los Angeles. A year later they moved back to Cleveland because, they claimed, they could not make any friends there. The truth was that they had been just as unsuccessful in making friends in Cleveland.

Friendliness is a reflection of qualities that lie deep inside. It cannot be counterfeited. An explorer I know found friendly people at the equator and in an outpost not far from the North Pole. I have found friendly people in a small village in Montana and in New York City. The size or the climate of a place has nothing to do with friendliness. A location cannot make people friendly if they are not naturally so. If it could, perhaps we could end our society's troubles—maybe even eliminate war—by moving everyone there.

By the way, don't jump to conclusions about the friendliness or unfriendliness of a town. It is an established fact that certain changes in weather can make people uncomfortable and irritable, and hence unfriendly. That, however, is only a temporary condition. It is also possible that people will seem unfriendly just because they are reserved. They may become surprisingly helpful when there is an emergency or disaster, even under the worst weather conditions. And people who seem reserved, even cold, when you first meet them may eventually become the warmest of friends.

Entertaining

As often as not, big cocktail parties turn out to be boring because people make a great display of what a good time they're having even when they aren't. Having a few friends in is relaxing, though, and offers the opportunity for pleasant and easygoing conversation.

If you are in a position to give dinners for friends, limit the number of people to six so that they can be seated at one table. This number and arrangement makes for convenient eating and all-around friendly conversation. Even a simple meal, served under such conditions, will be enjoyed by all.

If you can afford it and want a big crowd, hire a hall and make it a banquet. It will relieve you of all responsibility, put each guest on his or her own, and save you a lot of work.

GRANDCHILDREN

This is a touchy, dangerous subject for an outsider to discuss. However, since I have nine grandchildren, permit me to speak for myself. What I have learned as a grandfather, plus what I have been told by other grandparents, may be enlightening.

It is beneficial for my wife's health for her to live in southern Florida; therefore, we are located 1,355 miles from our grandchildren, and we do miss them very much. We have found that most retired grandparents who have moved far away from their grandchildren miss them just as much.

When a man retires he has many important decisions to make, and the love he and his wife have for their grandchildren should not be a decisive factor in whether or not they should move to another location. I have known grandparents who stayed where they were, only to see their sons or sons-in-law transferred by their companies to another city. The grandparents were able and willing to move to that other city, but there was no guarantee against still other transfers in a year or perhaps five years.

Large corporations today have branch offices, factories, and warehouses in various parts of this country, and even in foreign countries. Employees, especially those in executive positions, are often transferred to other locations, sometimes on short notice. The corporations even arrange to take over the sale of homes of men who are transferred and pay the moving expenses. If the sale of those homes results in a loss, the corporations make up the difference. So transfers are made very attractive to young executives on the way up, and you can hardly expect your children to forgo their opportunities.

I also know of cases where a son or son-in-law decided to work for another company in another city. Some couples change jobs and move several times.

Well, we just can't have everything, and no matter what we do some kind of price tag is involved. It is usually up to us to decide whether we are willing to pay that price.

There are grandparents who miss their grandchildren so much that they commute back and forth to visit them—whether they're commuting from Miami Beach, San Diego, or Hong Kong. That's fine if you can afford it. But there are other, less costly things you can do besides commuting back and forth:

Take a trip to where they live. This will give you a change of scenery and offer you plenty of time to visit with your grandchildren. As after any vacation, you will be glad to get back home.

Have them visit you. If your children cannot afford the expense, pay the cost of your grandchildren's visit. This gives them a chance to travel, which all children enjoy, and if they behave while staying with you, you will have a ball. If they misbehave, you won't be too sorry to see them leave.

Take them on a trip. If you have any kind of camper or trailer, not only can you visit your grandchildren periodically but you can take them on trips. Children particularly enjoy camping in the woods, especially near a lake or river. If you provide this treat, they'll think you the greatest grandparents in the world and love you dearly because of it.

It's nice to send gifts—especially if you live a long distance away from your grandchildren and aren't always with them on special occasions like birthdays. The gifts will please them, and you will probably receive a card or letter of thanks. But how can grandchildren, especially during their formative years, get to know you if you do not see them often enough? Sending gifts cannot accomplish that, because gifts are soon forgotten—sometimes in a matter of days.

However, your grandchildren will not so readily forget the things you do *with* them and *for* them—which is only possible if you are there in person. A camping trip, particularly, is something they will remember and talk about for years. Information and comments on campers, motor homes, and travel trailers are available in Appendix H ("Recreational Vehicles").

If you live very near your grandchildren, you may be tempted to visit them nearly every day—but you need not, and really should not, visit grandchildren too often. When you do, it is advisable not to spend too much time with them if it makes you overtired or grouchy. Children can be unruly, and they have seemingly unlimited endurance. Fortunately, except when you are baby-sitting, you are in a position to walk out and go back to the quiet of your own home.

On the subject of baby-sitting: Some grandparents enjoy it, others do not. In either case, if you live where your grandchildren are, you will be called upon to baby-sit, usually on the pretext that it isn't easy these days to get reliable baby-sitters—not that your son, son-in-law, daughter, or daughter-in-law wants to *impose* on you.

If you do baby-sit for your grandchildren and know how to get along with them (by giving of *yourself,* not gifts), they may form an attachment that will be deeply gratifying to you for the rest of your life. And should you really need them later, when they have grown up and you have grown older, they will be happy to do what they can for you.

This chapter has dealt with the subject of avoiding loneliness. Before leaving this topic, I'd like to point out the vast difference between *loneliness* and *being alone.* Everyone needs to be alone occasionally. It is sad if we cannot find comfort and a measure of enjoyment in our own company. Retirement gives us time for that pleasure.

Don't Be Idle

THE greatest danger in retirement is that it offers the opportunity to do nothing. For physical health we need physical activity, and for mental health we need mental activity. Idleness is not good for anyone, whether retired or not. Sailors and prisoners have their time pretty well routinized for them, but both have large amounts of unused hours. Sailors are kept busy scrubbing the decks and polishing brass; prisoners, if nothing else, break big rocks into little ones.

If *anybody* has the chance to do nothing, it will be the astronauts when they make that trip to Mars and back. To accomplish a landing on Mars and return to Earth will require about 700 days, almost two years. There probably won't be any serious trouble getting there and back. The real big problem, according to experts, will be to keep those astronauts busy, to protect them from the malady of doing nothing.

Gerontologists make a study of the changes that result from aging. Most of them agree that a lack of physical and mental activity shortens a person's life. You really were a busy man when you were working at those old jobs of yours, but in spite of that you managed to find plenty of time to do other things. Why? Because your life had organization and you had a sense of time. No wonder it is said that if you want something done, ask a busy man to do it.

When a man reaches 65 and retires, he goes from an active life into a life that is basically inactive. His previous life had organization, and time meant something. His new life lacks organization, and time now may seem meaningless. There's too much of it. And when there is too much of anything, it loses its value.

The retired man is suddenly isolated from the activities, the responsibilities, and the people that absorbed his time and energies, and he now has the problem of avoiding an empty and lonely life. If he doesn't solve that problem, he may lose complete confidence in himself.

Doing nothing is relaxing when it has been earned, but you have to earn such interludes constantly; you can't rest on past performances. The person you hurt most by doing nothing is yourself. Sure, you earned the right to be idle, but what good is free time if you don't know how to use it?

Shakespeare said that cowards die many times before their death. So do retired people, if they do nothing but sit around and think about it.

Doing nothing gives a person too much time to look back. When you reflect on the past, you realize how the time has flown and how little time there is left.

With that comes regret for the things you *could* have done—last week, last month, last year. When a person has nothing to do, he doesn't think of what he has accomplished, but rather of what he missed. He will also recall all the mistakes he made—or thinks he made. But he is making the biggest mistake of his life *now,* when he is retired, by doing nothing. Doing nothing amounts to killing time, and that is a crime you are committing against yourself.

If you sit at home doing nothing you get cabin fever, a fever that aspirin can't control. Don't call your doctor; not even he can help you. The only person who can help you is *yourself.* Cabin fever is what people up in the Yukon get. It's caused by the boredom and frustration felt in remote places where companions and activities are very limited.

Doing nothing leads to boredom, and boredom brings a fatigue that rest will not relieve. That kind of fatigue will interfere with your sleep, because how can anyone have a good night's sleep if he has sat around and rested all day? The longer you stay in bed the next morning, the more you will yawn all day and the more tired and exhausted you'll be. You will reach a point where going to the store for a loaf of bread will seem like a big effort.

Get enough of that boredom and you'll think you are sick. If you confess that to your doctor, he will do one of three things: give you a prescription for some useless pills, chase you out for wasting his time, or tell you to get busy and find something to do that will keep you occupied and interested.

Alligators and crocodiles lie around doing nothing most of the time, but they have a good reason: By pretending to be asleep they fool other animals into thinking it's safe to come close. If they come close enough—well, that's the next meal.

It can be helpful, on occasion, to recall our sorrows and failures, but it's a terrible mistake to feel sorry for ourselves. Instead, we would do well to emphasize the positive and realize that somehow or other we've managed to overcome various difficulties in our life. All living things must adjust to changing conditions in order to survive. We got this far, and now we have to figure out how to continue to live useful, satisfying lives.

Now that you're retired, *you* are the master of your time. You have the opportunity to use it wisely. Don't throw that opportunity away.

If your wife has not worked—at least not in recent years—she is a victim of your retirement. It is you and you alone who have retired; your wife did not. *Her job goes on just as before.* In fact, she has to work harder if you sit around the house all day. She not only has to ask you what you would like for dinner, but now she has to ask what you want for *lunch.*

Another thing: If you sit around the house all day, whether you do something or nothing, the result is the wrong kind of togetherness. Like a mote in the eye or a pebble in the shoe, small annoyances create great irritations. The result may be nasty quarrels, which sometimes lead to complete alienation.

As we get older, all of us get more firmly set in our habits. But if you can think of retirement as a fresh start, you should be able to shift away from some of your accustomed ways of doing things. Somebody once said, "Today is the first day of the rest of your life." Think about that. What can it mean for you?

Make it mean something for your wife as well as for yourself. Don't expect her to change if you can't. She isn't used to having you around all day, and you shouldn't expect her to give up all her time to keep you company or wait on you.

The only person who can help a retired person escape from "solitary confinement" is himself; no one else can do it for him. The only way to escape (and this requires an easy but firm decision) is to exert the physical and mental energy to keep active. There are an infinite number of ways to keep busy, from the least demanding (watching television, for example) to physically taxing exercises and a full-time job. Two types of activities—jobs and travel—are such large subjects that they are treated as separate chapters in this book.

As long as a retired person is active, he will enjoy freedom. Growing older can slow him down a little physically, but he can learn something new at any age. Experts on aging confirm that repeatedly.

KEEPING PHYSICALLY ACTIVE

Lack of exercise is not conducive to general good health at any age. Now that you are retired, not only do you have the time for exercise but it is even more essential that you engage in some form of it. To retain or to improve your health, you must exercise. To get energy, you must expend it.

Exercise is good for the circulation. It conditions

the heart and allows it to work more slowly and more efficiently. It acts as a good laxative; it is an excellent tonic for the arteries, and a wonderful pump for the lungs. It is one of the best tranquilizers for the relief of tensions and the best antidote for insomnia. And there's one surprising and rewarding thing about exercise: The more of it you do, the more you will be able to do in time.

Too many people exercise too little. Some exercise too soon after a heavy meal. Others exercise too much—even to the point of fatigue. We need rest just as much as we need exercise. Overdoing either one is not good for us and takes away from both the benefits and the pleasures.

Do not engage in any exercise without a physical checkup by your doctor. He can tell you which form of exercise would be good for you, how much, and how often. In some cases he will tell you to exercise in a limited and special way.

The first thing we do in the morning is get out of bed. Now here is a simple little exercise you can do to start the day. Before getting up, stretch. Take it easy and don't knock a joint out of place. Watch a cat and note how it stretches whenever it wakes up. All animals instinctively stretch after a sleep. Animals know how to take care of themselves, and we can learn a lot by watching them.

In a heart test of the men who operate the double-decker buses in London, it was found that the bus drivers tended to have more heart attacks than the conductors. The reason given—which seems obvious—was that the conductors had to walk up and down stairs to get to the upper deck and back.

This suggests another simple exercise. Stairs are available almost everywhere. Walk up and down them every chance you get instead of using the elevator. That does not mean you should walk up to the twenty-fifth floor—although you may be able to do that in time.

One of the harmful things you can do to your body is to sit or stand in one place too long. Just remember the coffee breaks at the place where you worked, and at least treat yourself to one if you do not want to do anything else. There are, however, certain other breaks or little forms of exercise you can do as a relief from constant sitting or standing.

You can walk around the room several times, stretch, and drop something on the floor and pick it up. (Do not stoop forward to pick it up; bend your knees to protect your back.) Even better, take a walk around the block. If you want a drink of water, go and get it yourself instead of asking someone to bring it to you.

No doubt you have heard, or read, that on a long trip in a car, experts recommend getting out now and then to walk, stretch, run, jump—or do something else active—for mental and physical relief *and for safety.*

One of the reasons, they say, that some people get physically upset by long airplane trips is the time zone changes. It is further said that those trips cause fatigue in a clinical way that is not fully understood. But we do know that sitting in a confined space too long and overeating and overdrinking contribute to the problem. The new giant jets may well remedy that. There is not only room enough to take a walk and stretch, but there is even a flight of stairs a person could climb at least every hour.

Sports offer an enjoyable way of getting physical exercise. But some sports are deceptive in this regard. Consider golf, which seems to be one of the most popular sports for older people. Warm-climate areas and retirement communities make a big thing of their golf facilities because they know well that most men look forward to playing golf when they retire. There are lots of advantages to playing golf: It gets you out of the house, it's relaxing (if you don't get too emotional about it), and you meet and mix with other people and perhaps form friendships. But golf is not considered to be good exercise because the action is too slow. If you ride in a golf cart, it is even less of an exercise.

Incidentally, if you play golf every day it can become more of a task than a pleasure, and you will need something else to do for relaxation. Even playing golf can become routine. Any sport, in fact, gets boring if you engage in it too often.

Bowling is a good form of exercise. A feature that is both an advantage and a disadvantage is that it is played indoors. Although you don't have the pleasure of being outdoors, bowling can be played in any kind of weather, and you don't have to wait for the ninth hole to get a cup of coffee. Also, bowling is not expensive, and the ball you play with is too big to get lost. That alone saves you money and aggravation.

Horseshoe pitching is enjoyable and is good exercise. It costs only a few dollars at most and gets you outdoors.

But there are other, more vigorous forms of exercise that are considerably more beneficial. Here are three that are all highly rated by the experts: swimming, bicycle riding, and walking. Note that swimming heads the list. It is considered to be the very best all-around exercise there is, and the amount of exertion you are able or willing to put into it is up to you. If you don't think you can ride a bicycle, try a tricycle. Many older people have used them and find it both pleasant and a good form of transportation.

Third on the experts' list is walking, but it should be done at a brisk pace. When you walk briskly, the exercise of the legs helps the circulation of your blood and is good for your heart. If you cannot walk at a brisk pace, then walk slowly. Done with regularity, walking qualifies as exercise. It can be done by anyone, anywhere, and requires no special equipment besides comfortable shoes that give proper support.

Walking for exercise (especially a brisk walk) is best taken alone. When you walk with someone, conversation slows you down. So does concern for your companion, if that person can't walk as fast as you.

If you live where it is hot during the middle hours of the day (especially during the summer), take your walk or do other exercises in the early morning or late afternoon. The heart works ten times harder at 90 degrees than it does at 70.

I have seen people drive their cars around the corner to buy a newspaper or a pack of cigarettes. *Walk* there. If you don't want to walk, use a bicycle. Your automobile can be your worst enemy if it keeps you from exercising your legs. The longer you ride everywhere in your automobile and delay walking or other exercise involving legwork, the sooner you will be taken for a ride in another automobile—a hearse.

Finally, there is a form of exercise that is a favorite among many retired people: dancing. There are numerous different dances that you and your wife can learn and master—from waltzes to tangos to square dance steps. Many communities that cater to retired people have clubs or hotels with live bands, and it is usually easy to find a dance instructor.

HOBBIES

"Get a hobby" is the advice often given to retired people and those facing retirement. Well, what is a hobby? Dictionary definitions emphasize that it is any absorbing activity that a person enjoys and can pursue during leisure time. A hobby is a diversion, an avocation.

If you had a hobby during your working years, you will probably look forward to spending more time at it now, particularly if you have developed some real skills. That puts you ahead of the game, but it isn't wise to devote all your time and energies to it, because it isn't a hobby anymore if it crowds out other interests, friends, exercise, and travel. Then it stops being relaxing, and you will have to find something else to distract you from it.

Winston Churchill and President Eisenhower were two famous Sunday painters who spent many hours at their hobby after retirement, but Churchill continued to travel and to write, and Eisenhower kept busy seeing friends and playing golf.

You may be so good at your hobby that you can get paid for your work. There are two ways to look at this possibility. On the one hand, you can consider turning it into a full-time operation. You have to be objective in trying to decide whether you enjoy it enough for that, and whether you hold your own with the competition. If so, fine. But if you don't want to put that much into it, you can work as much or as little as you wish and consider as gravy any payment you receive for selling something you have made or for performing a service. You will get a lot of satisfaction from knowing that someone admired a table you made—or a picture you painted or a rock garden you set up or a lamp you wired—enough to want one for himself.

If you don't already have a hobby, perhaps there is something you have always wanted to try but never got around to for one reason or another. This is the time. If the hobby of your choice involves expensive equipment or materials, join a group where you can use their equipment and where you may be able to buy materials in small quantities, perhaps at a discount. If there is no such group, try to rent the equipment or make do with what you have until you know for certain that the activity is not beyond your ability and will hold your interest.

What if you want a hobby and are no more inclined toward one than another? Try to select something that is suitable to your aptitudes and your pocketbook. (Some hobbies can be extremely expensive.) Visit your local hardware or department store, especially if it has a hobby section. Check the Yellow Pages of your telephone book for hobby and model shops, and watch your local newspapers for announcements of hobby shows and amateur competitions.

A helpful and interesting booklet, *How to Find a Hobby,* can be obtained from Richard Gordon Byrne, 7120 Newburgh Road, Evansville, Ind. 47715. Send 25¢ in coins with a stamped, self-addressed *long* envelope. Mr. Byrne has another booklet with a complete list of up-to-date books on hobbies together with a list of selected magazines and hobby associations. If you write to him for this booklet, be sure to include a list of the hobbies you are interested in and send another 25¢ with a stamped, self-addressed *long* envelope.

A free booklet, *The Great World of Hobbies,* is available from Hobby Industry of America, Inc., 200 Fifth Avenue, New York, N.Y. 10010.

You may also get some ideas from visiting the arts and crafts shops of Sun City, Arizona.

Hobbies that keep a person isolated from others for long periods of time can become boring. Perhaps you can share a workshop with a friend or neighbor or spend at least part of your time in a crafts center if there is one in your community. You might even consider moving to a place like Sun City where you can pursue your hobby in a professionally equipped shop or studio. In addition, many others will be working there, which minimizes the chance of conflict and brings together people with mutual interests. There will be breaks for conversation and an opportunity to develop friendships. There is far less chance of losing interest in a hobby when it is shared by others working on the same or other hobbies.

If you choose a hobby and then find it uninteresting or want to discontinue it for some other reason, try another hobby, or several of them, before you completely give up the idea of having one.

If you think you are too old to start a hobby, allow me to remind you that Grandma Moses (Anna Mary Robertson), who never had an art lesson, started painting when she was 78—and working at her hobby and keeping busy with other things undoubtedly helped her to live to 101 years of age.

Travel is a great hobby, and retired people should indulge in it as much as possible. Travel is such an interesting and enjoyable hobby that I have devoted a special chapter to the subject.

Hobbies can add much enjoyment to your retirement years. But don't think a hobby is a rope that will pull you out of the depression that retirement can bring. You need a lot more than a rope.

Have a hobby if you want one, *but keep it a hobby*. In that way—and that way only—it will give you great interest and relaxation. Then, in addition, be active in other spheres and meet and mix with other people.

OTHER WAYS TO KEEP BUSY

There are many other, less-organized ways of pleasurably spending your time. Taking a walk, a long walk, is something you can do alone. It is not only good exercise, as I said, but it is also a great tonic, a way to clear your mind. Taking a morning walk every day is what kept President Harry S. Truman in wonderful condition for many years. If you like order and routine, you might like to take the same walk each day. You can time yourself if you are doing it for exercise, and you might like the idea of using a pedometer to keep track of how far you go. Or you might want to cover a different part of your town or surrounding countryside each day to familiarize yourself with it.

Try feeding the pigeons in the park. After awhile

you will single out certain pigeons, and some of them
will get to know you. Watching their behavior can be
fascinating. You might also put a feeder station in a
tree near one of the windows of your house. Bird
watching is an extremely popular activity and can be
done on the spur of the moment or on special trips with
binoculars. You will find many other people who share
this interest, and it may lead you to read up on different
species.

If there's a zoo in your city, go there occasionally.
It is often more interesting to watch animals than people. If you have grandchildren, take them along. If you
do not have grandchildren, volunteer to take someone
else's children, perhaps from an orphanage. You would
do well, however, to get to know the children before
you attempt such an outing, because if they are not
well behaved or at least willing to cooperate with you,
the outing could be more than you can handle, or at
least it might not be much fun for you.

I feel sorry for anyone who does not enjoy reading. If reading has been a part of your life, you will
surely use your new-found time to catch up on the
books you have long wanted to get to and couldn't. Just
don't let it keep you from other activities. If you haven't
been a reader, now is the time to start. If you want
some guidance in making your selections, don't be
hesitant about talking it over with the librarian, and
ask other people for their recommendations.

Your library, incidentally, will have current newspapers and periodicals on hand, and is a good place to
spend a rainy afternoon. Some libraries even lend records and films for home use.

Going to watch sporting activities is a pleasant,

even exciting way to pass the time. Not many communities have a large stadium, but almost every town has local amateur teams, and all college towns have some sort of competitive athletic programs. Even high school games can be exciting, especially if you know some of the players or if you ever played the game yourself when you were a youngster. If there are no spectator sports at all where you live, make a one-day excursion now and then to see a game in a nearby city. Just watching the crowd is interesting.

The trouble with card playing is that people become addicted, even if they don't gamble. Most bridge players, for example, get so carried away that they play for hours and hours on end. If you have never played cards, some games can easily and quickly be learned (although bridge is not one of them) and you can pass the time pleasantly this way. If you don't like cards, there is almost always a bingo game to be found in a church or community house.

If your city offers a program in adult education, take advantage of it. There is no reason to retire from learning just because you've retired from working. Now is your opportunity to satisfy your curiosity on almost any subject. Some cities and communities even offer special programs for the elderly. For example, the May 31, 1974, issue of *The New York Times* describes the Institute of Study for Older Adults, which offers courses on art, music, psychology, and many other subjects to people in 54 retirement homes and centers for the elderly in the Greater New York area. The oldest graduate of the institute—Joseph Schoenberger, 100, a retired diamond setter—recently completed courses on "Aging in Other Societies" and "Current Issues: Watergate."

You can also learn to play a musical instrument, speak a new language, or, as mentioned earlier, do some new dance steps. Such lessons are often free, and if a fee is charged it is usually small.

By keeping active you'll sleep better, feel better, and enjoy your meals more. You won't be inclined to sleep late because you'll have a reason to get up, something to look forward to. And you'll be surprised to learn that you won't have feelings of tiredness, the kind that lodge in the head rather than in the body. Reading or watching television in the evening will be more enjoyable, interesting, and relaxing after spending the day at some outside activity. You won't go to bed too early and spend a restless night.

A wonderful thing about retirement is that it offers marvelous opportunities for variety. If you spread your branches of activity, the roots of satisfaction will grow to their outer limits. You will have confidence in yourself, and you will feel wanted and needed. You will radiate cheerfulness and goodwill, qualities that attract both young and old people to you. Your children and grandchildren will enjoy your get-togethers more.

When your interests are varied, new facets of your personality will shine. Your wife too will be stimulated by your activities. Not only will the two of you have more to talk about, but you may even get her to join you in some of them. If, when all is said and done, you are not interested in outside activities, switch roles with your wife—you do the housework and let her retire. Maybe this will be her opportunity to find new stimulation. That may be what you need to get started.

To Move
or Not to Move?

THE first thing too many people do when they retire is move to another location. Why the rush? Now that they are retired, they finally have plenty of time to make this all-important decision.

Let's examine this subject of moving to another location.

Some people may want to move to an unusual place—for example, Barrow, Alaska, located above the Arctic Circle—which they may favor because of an interest in the Eskimos. Someone else, who is interested in penguins, would want to go to the Antarctic.

I can understand why the Eskimos would make for an interesting study. They manage to survive against great hardships and even enjoy themselves. As for penguins, they are friendly and make excellent neighbors. We could use many of them right here in this country.

But the fact is that most people are not conditioned mentally or physically for living in such unusual places.

WHAT ARE YOU RUNNING FROM?

If you are concerned about earthquakes, your best bet is to move to the southwestern section of Alabama, the extreme northwestern or the southern section of Florida, the extreme southeastern section of Mississippi, or the southeastern section of Texas. These areas are the only ones in the United States where there is no reasonable expectation of an earthquake.

Does lightning frighten you? Then you had better go to the place where there is only one thunderstorm a year: San Diego, California.

Because we live in a huge country with all types of topography and climate, there are other, quite common dangers: blizzards, droughts, dust storms, floods, forest fires (brush and grass), hurricanes, landslides, sandstorms, tidal waves, and tornados.

Of course, the automobile should be added to the list. More than 55,000 people were killed and more than four million injured in automobile accidents in 1973. To escape that danger, go where you are welcome but your car is not. Your best bet is Mackinac Island, Michigan.

How about intercontinental ballistic missiles, nuclear war? Your best bet is northern Canada—Flin Flon, Manitoba; Grand Prairie, Alberta; Prince Albert, Saskatchewan; or Prince George, British Columbia.

Now that we are aware of pollution and its dangers to human comfort and health, it has become a factor in making people decide to move from one area to another. But it is difficult to find any place, short of an uninhabited wilderness, that is completely free of it. Few of us would want to, or could, live in such a place anyway. Of course, if we all moved into some wilderness, it would soon become polluted too. There is pollution now even on the moon in the form of litter sent there via missiles and left there by the astronauts, including a few golf balls.

In addition to air pollution, we now have polluted rivers, lakes, bays, oceans, and soil. Noise is also considered a serious form of pollution. Polluters include industrial plants and public utilities; automobiles, buses, taxis, and trucks; and insecticides and pesticides, which pollute not only the air but the soil and plants, including foods.

The beach at Santa Barbara, California, was polluted badly by an oil spill from an offshore oil well. Phoenix, Arizona, was polluted by copper smelters more than 50 miles away. And we all know of the smog over Los Angeles and New York City.

Mackinac Island in Michigan is the only place we can escape the commonest contributor to air pollution, the automobile.

It is important to recognize that many communities are doing something to fight pollution. Eventually they will succeed. The dirty, noisy city you leave may clean up its pollution sooner than the city to which you are planning to move.

Before you run from a city because of its pollution problem—or any other problem, for that matter—check to see whether the people are forming an organization and dedicating themselves to correcting the condition. In San Francisco and neighboring cities, some of the people formed an organization to fight encroachment on their remaining bay lands—and they won.

A good place to live would be Santa Fe, the capital of New Mexico. It has a population of only 39,207 (1970), and there are many attractions. But, like every other place, it has a drawback: Its altitude is 6,950 feet, so it would not do for some people, especially those with heart conditions or high blood pressure or who are anemic.

Here are five major cities in warm-climate areas that are virtually free of air pollution. The population figures are from the 1970 census.

> Phoenix, Ariz.: 581,562
> Tucson, Ariz.: 262,933
> San Diego, Calif.: 696,769
> Miami, Fla.: 334,859
> St. Petersburg, Fla.: 216,232

The air in Miami is rated among this country's purest, but that air is becoming polluted by the steadily increasing number of automobiles, buses, taxis, and trucks—the same way every city with such heavy traffic is afflicted.

Before you move to avoid a particular danger, remember that there is even danger in your own home. Ask any doctor, hospital, or insurance company. And moving to another location exposes you to a new sort of danger—the danger that your hopes and expectations will not be met. This is especially true if you rush into it. Let us consider the many reasons for this.

Sooner or later, you may find that you need *more*

than just a place to live if you want to enjoy your retirement. If you move to another location, you may miss the companionship of old friends, your children, and especially your grandchildren. This alone can keep you from enjoying the place you move to. Then there is the adjustment any move requires. Some older people need to be in familiar surroundings; it is difficult for them to adjust to a new location. We could be happy even in Timbuktu if we could take along the friends and family we love and transplant our favorite comforts and amusements and weather.

WHAT ARE YOU LOOKING FOR?

But let's get down to basics. The expense of moving and setting up a new apartment or home in these highly inflated times has to be considered. It generally far exceeds the expected cost. Instead of moving, perhaps you would do better to use that money for a prolonged vacation or trip—or a second honeymoon—and create some happy memories to enjoy in the years ahead. It is a safe investment, and it may prove to be one that will pay dividends as long as you live.

Weigh the advantages and disadvantages of moving to another location. If you postpone your decision, you may learn of a better place than the one you thought of first, or find some other good reason for changing your mind.

Many people favor a place that is noted for its beautiful scenery. Therefore, consider Lake Louise in Canada. Closed in by mountains on three sides, it is among the most scenic places in the world. But if you sit in a chair on the patio of the hotel facing the lake and do nothing else but look at it day after day, it can become extremely boring.

Let us also consider the question of crowds. A retired person often wants to move to a smaller city to avoid the congestion of a large one. It is possible, in this day and age, that the smaller city will be just as crowded for its size and facilities.

Then there is the retired man who wants to move to another location because he believes that the crime rate in his city is too high. He plans to move to Xville because he has heard that the crime rate there is very low. Before he moves to Xville he should write to the FBI and ask for figures on the per capita crime rate of his city and of Xville. The address is Federal Bureau of Investigation, Washington, D.C. 20530.

Now let us consider moving to a particular location because living costs are said to be lower there. If it costs less to live in a certain locality, you can bet that many others know this as well as you do. Soon enough, a lot of those others will also move there for the same reason. As that happens, prices go up; they always do under such conditions. Furthermore, if you are going to move to that locality because it costs less to live there, it might be advisable to take into consideration the cost of moving and the expense of setting up a new apartment or home.

If the pleasure of fishing is a factor in your choice, find out whether fish are still there. Pollution of one kind or another has killed them off in many formerly excellent fishing areas. And if fish are still there, find out whether they are safe to eat.

If golf is a decisive factor in choosing another location, remember that enjoying the game on weekends is no guarantee that you will enjoy it daily, or even several times a week. Playing a game on weekends can be an enjoyable and relaxing experience, but anything done too often may become another sort of job.

Be sure to check the taxes, especially in rapidly developing areas. It would be reasonable to expect that when more people move into a city, taxes would be lowered or at least remain stationary as a result of the additional tax money received from new residents. But it doesn't work that way.

An example will illustrate what happens. In a city I visited on various occasions, the parking meter rate was one cent for 12 minutes or five cents for an hour. That city experienced a great influx of new residents and with them an influx of automobiles. The first thing the city did was to install more meters. The 12 minutes for one cent was eliminated, and the rate jumped to five cents for 30 minutes, or ten cents for an hour. That's a 100 percent increase.

The officials of a city justify the need for increased revenue by claiming that as more people move into their city, they must add to the equipment and personnel of the fire department, the police department, and garbage collection and other services, and that often another school and, perhaps, an additional fire station must be built. There certainly is a basis for their claim. One way to avoid high prices and increased taxes is by not moving to a booming area.

The health factor induces some people to move.

But before you move to a location that you think will be better for some ailment you have or for other considerations affecting your health, check with your doctor.

Weather is important to everyone in one way or another. All retirees want to live in a place where there is good weather all year, and too many are led to believe that such a place exists. The areas with the least stormy weather are southern Arizona, California, and New Mexico, and each of those places has the added benefit of cool nights. (See the section on warm-climate areas later in this chapter.)

It may be that climate isn't as important a consideration to retired people as it seems at first. They have an advantage other people don't have: They can adjust their routines (except on rare occasions) to suit weather conditions anywhere, whereas people who must go out to their jobs—especially those who work outdoors—cannot.

Living in a large city has advantages as well as disadvantages. Give some thought to moving to a small town or to the country. Such locations may also have some disadvantages, but their many advantages are well worth considering under present conditions. In the past few years many corporations have moved their factories to smaller towns; some have even moved their executive offices there. Small towns—or the country—offer a better opportunity for the fine exercise of walking and other outdoor recreational activities. They also offer fresh air, less noise, no traffic jams, free parking, and lower-priced land on which to build. And you can always get to a big city in a hurry if necessary. In small towns, older people have a better chance to mix with younger people, and that is good for both of them. Generally, the people have more time and are therefore friendlier.

If you decide to move to a small town or to the country—in fact, wherever you plan to move—check on the ready availability of food and drug stores, doctor, dentist, hospital, and the fire department. Some people may want to consider the availability of part-time paid jobs, domestic help, or a library. It is also convenient—and often necessary—to have an airport within a reasonable distance.

Serious consideration must be given also to the matter of transportation, for the day may come when you are no longer able (or permitted) to drive a car. If you move to another state, that state may refuse to exchange your driver's license without a test, at least for eyesight, hearing, and the ability to read and understand traffic signs. Most states now have, or soon will have, reexamination tests for a driver's license every so many years.

Where shopping, doctors' offices, and amusement centers are not within walking distance, good, economical public transportation is a must. In this, large cities have greater advantages than country places or small towns. But in the home city, relatives or friends are available for transportation, and the retired person can arrange his time to suit their convenience. One or all of them will be immediately available in an emergency.

Don't let people who live somewhere else talk you into moving where they are. The natives generally praise the place, as grandparents praise their grandchildren. The fact that it is good for them is no guarantee

that it will be good for you. Having friends is important at any time of life and a necessity when a person
is retired, but even a friend shouldn't influence you to
move to where he is located. He may be genuinely concerned about your comfort and welfare, but what appeals to him as a place to live may not be at all suitable for you.

When a man retires, he should be the one to decide whether to move and where to move. The only
other person who should share in those decisions is his
wife. Do what is best for *you* and for your wife. Close
your ears to what all others say. What may not be the
right thing for others may be exactly the right thing
for you.

By all means, don't be lured by advertisements.
Even the devil could follow the example of some real
estate developers and place ads in newspapers or mail
out colorful brochures, showing how exciting life is in
hell. Before you move anywhere, *see the place* if you
have not already done so. Such a trip may cost much
less than making another move.

A great deal of information about a specific place
can be secured by checking an atlas, an almanac, and
an encyclopedia. If you do not have them handy, go to
a library. Another source of information is the state
in which you are interested. Appendix A gives a list
of the state capitals and their zip codes. You may want
to write to the Department of Tourism, the Department of Commerce, the Department of Labor, the Department of Taxation, or the Department of Transportation, depending on the type of information you are
seeking.

If you are interested in a special city, you can gather much valuable and useful information about it by getting a copy of its newspaper. To obtain the names and addresses of the newspapers of a great many cities, go to your telephone company and consult the out-of-town directories. Most cities include these in the Yellow Pages of their telephone books. Look under the heading "Newspapers." After you get the name and address, you can get the zip code number from your post office. Write to the paper and ask which of their issues features large display advertisements for supermarkets, which features the real estate section, and the price for each. Where more than one newspaper is listed in the Yellow Pages of the telephone book, it may be advisable to write to each of them.

When you are scouting for a place to live, be leery of any area where there are a lot of real estate brokers. Although this indicates that a lot of people are moving *into* that area, it also indicates that others are moving *out*—and putting their homes up for sale.

Be especially wary of any new development—any area, in fact—in which too many of the homes are tagged with for-sale signs. Let's be rational: All those homes are being offered for sale for some good reason. The people living in these homes know all about the area.

A Trial Period

If there is one thing you, as a retired man, have plenty of, it is time. Use some portion of that time to decide whether the place you plan to move to is the right one for you. You can do that by living there for a trial period before you make your decision to move there permanently.

Retired people who want to move to a new location for any reason, and especially because of the weather, will find it a distinct advantage to live there during that area's worst season. In the North, that would be during the winter, and in warm-climate areas that would certainly be during the long, hot summers. Yes, it is easy to escape the heat with the aid of air conditioning—but if you are going to live in a warm-climate area, you surely will want to spend a lot of your time outdoors. At any rate, it is best to disregard what others say about the weather and really find out whether *you* can be comfortable in it.

A trial period will also give you a chance to find out whether there are political, social, and other factors that you cannot adjust to or will not want to adjust to. And, of more importance, you will have the opportunity—by personal experience—to learn *the cost of living* there.

Two aspects of health that are not related to medical factors deserve special mention. The first is that pulling up roots and settling in a new location may depress some people, and a real state of depression can affect health. A doctor can confirm that, and he need not be a psychiatrist to do it.

The second is the importance of knowing what a person finds interesting and enjoys doing. This subject is explored more fully in other chapters, but I mention it here because interest and enjoyment in themselves promote good health by giving meaning to life. It is very important to find out whether a new location provides the activities that satisfy these needs.

During that trial period it will not be advisable to buy a lot, a home, or a condominium. The wise thing to do is to rent an apartment or live in a hotel, an efficiency, or, if necessary, a furnished room. Some people will want to consider the idea of living in a mobile home during the trial period. For information and comment on mobile homes, see Appendix G.

So do invest in a trial period. It may enable you to make the right decision—a decision that will pay you enjoyable living dividends for the rest of your life.

Some Things to Consider

If you think you really know where you want to settle, you may be tempted by an alluring ad for an apartment in a condominium. The advertisements do indeed make everything look very attractive. Before you make your decision, be sure to check on whether you are being asked to sign a Land Lease or a Recreation Lease, and find out whether there is a Management Fee and a Management Contract. Any or all of these can add to your costs. It's best to have the professional help of a lawyer, who can analyze all the fine print before you put your signature to a lease or contract.

To help you make a decision, here is a book by Carl Norcross, a housing market analyst who was formerly editor of *House & Home* magazine: *Townhouses and Condominiums: Residents' Likes and Dislikes*, published by the Urban Land Institute, 1200 18th Street, N.W., Washington, D.C. 20036. The price is $16.50, for which the book will be sent airmail.

Insurance is a special consideration. Persons who buy a condominium unit may want "Loss Assessments Coverage" in addition to the protection provided by the Condominium Association's insurance. A complete explanation of this type of insurance is clearly given in a free brochure made available by Allstate Insurance Companies. If you can't get to a sales office of Allstate or to a Sears building, write to Allstate at P.O. Box 236, Northbrook, Ill. 60062.

If you carry homeowner's insurance with a company other than Allstate, ask that company whether it issues such insurance.

If you have decided to buy in the country—whether you're buying a lot to build on, a house, or even a second home for weekends, vacations, or other recreational use—do consider the purchase of some extra land. Just be sure that the land is fertile. A running stream or a good well on the property is especially valuable.

Plant a few fruit trees on that extra land if none are there.

During an inflationary period, you can always grow your own vegetables, have some chickens, maybe a few pigs or lambs, cows or goats for milk, several beehives, or raise some of your own beef. You can even have a pony or two for your grandchildren, and a horse for yourself and others.

If you own a second home—or even a mobile home, camper, motor home, or travel trailer—you can rent it to other people when you are not using it. Not only will this provide extra income, but under certain arrangements you can also have the advantage of a tax-deduction allowance. Ask an accountant or tax consultant to explain what arrangements must be made to support your claim.

RETIREMENT COMMUNITIES

A retirement community will give you the advantage of living among people who not only are of your age group but are also, like yourself, retired—and that makes for mutual respect and understanding. If you desire the company of young people or children, you can volunteer to do some social work that will put you in contact with them.

Where there is discontent in such communities, it is generally because there isn't enough to do. In fact, in some places there is *nothing* to do. If you are interested in retirement-community living you should consider the communities that offer a variety of activities. There are a number of them that do.

Sun City, 13 miles northwest of Phoenix, Arizona, greatly impressed me. Here is what this community offers:

Entertainment. Nationally known bands, classical music, and performances by stars from the theater, movies, and television. Also dancing, card playing, and a theater group for residents interested in participating in such an activity.

Sports. Four 18-hole golf courses with low annual rates, four heated swimming pools, tennis, lawn bowling, shuffleboard, billiards, and boating and fishing on a 33-acre lake.

Workshops. Arts and crafts of many kinds at four professionally equipped shops and studios.

Travel. Group trips at reduced rates.

An annual charge of $20 is made for each person to cover all of Sun City's recreational activities except golf. Should such a place appeal to you, there is one important point to consider: It attracts the kind of people who have the interest to participate in some or all of the activities being offered. An added plus is the friendships that are built with the people who share the interests.

Sun City also has four medical and dental centers, its own six-story modern hospital, eight churches, four shopping centers with more than 165 stores, and nine restaurants. In addition to an indoor theater, it has a 7,500-seat outdoor amphitheater.

There are homes, duplexes, and garden apartments to house its population of 23,000, which keeps growing. Like Phoenix and Tucson, Sun City has long, hot summers, but the climate is dry and the heat is therefore not oppressive.

For further information write to Del E. Webb Retirement Community, 13813 Del Webb Boulevard, Sun City, Ariz. 85351.

There is another Sun City near Riverside, California, and a Sun City Center about 30 miles south of Tampa, Florida. I do not know what activities they offer, since I have not visited them. They are much smaller in size and scope than Sun City, Arizona. If you are interested in Sun City Center near Tampa, write for information to Walter-Gould, Inc., 5415 Mariner Street, Tampa, Fla. 33609. For information on the one near Riverside, write to Del E. Webb Corporation, 3800 N. Central Avenue, Phoenix, Ariz. 85012.

In addition to the Sun Cities, there are other communities that offer similar activities. Generally they are incorporated, and you can therefore secure their names and addresses by writing to the secretary of state, at the state's capital city, of any state in which you are interested. (See Appendix A for a list of the states and their capitals.)

It is not advisable to commit yourself to moving to a retirement community without going to see it personally and investigating everything about it and the area in which it is located. Here, again, is good reason for taking a trip when you retire, if you did not have the time to do that before your retirement. You should not only see the place to which you are thinking of moving, but should take advantage of the chance to see other places that may prove far more appealing.

Even if you have visited a place several times and feel it meets with your complete approval, you should still live there for a trial period before you move. In Sun City, Arizona, for example, there are apartments. Try to rent one during that trial period. Or, like everywhere else, you may find some homes up for sale. Try to rent one for several months (or even a year) with an option to buy it.

WARM-CLIMATE AREAS

Warm-climate areas are sections of this country where the winters are generally warm or mild, including desert, tropical, or subtropical areas. The warm-climate areas do have their long, hot summers—they must, if they are to have their pleasant, warm climate in the winter—but thanks to air conditioning, it is now possible to live in comfort in warm-climate areas all year round.

Life may be more easygoing in a warm climate,

but such climates do limit our activities. A too-hot or too-bright sun is unpleasant for some people. There is also the question of humidity. Humidity is a measure of the moisture content of the atmosphere and is a factor in determining climate. Extremes of humidity affect personal comfort as greatly as extremes of temperature. If there is too much humidity, any activity, even walking, can be very tiring—especially for older people.

The atmosphere in desert areas is mostly very dry. The atmosphere in areas near large bodies of water with in-shore winds usually has a high humidity (except in high-altitude areas). There are ways to relieve these extreme conditions. If you live in a dry area, install a humidifier to add moisture to the atmosphere in your house. A dehumidifier will do the job if you live in an area with high humidity.

If you plan to move to a warm-climate area because it will prolong your life, forget it, unless you have some ailment that makes it advisable or necessary. According to the U.S. Census Bureau, people who live in the upper midwest states live longer than those in warm areas. The place where people live longest is a section of Nebraska where the temperature drops to well below zero in winter and in summer may go above 100 degrees.

Fundamentally, the important thing is not how long we live, but whether we find interest and enjoyment in living. The giant tortoise of the Galápagos Islands lives well over a hundred years, but who would want to be a Galápagos tortoise?

Don't fool yourself into believing that it costs less to live in warm-climate areas. Those days are gone. Because many other people have moved there, costs have gone way up. Prices used to be more reasonable during the summer in such areas, but the increasing number of summer tourists put an end to that. Hotel rates are, of course, lower during the summer, but that doesn't help the year-round residents.

In some warm-climate areas you will save money on heating bills, but that saving may largely be lost by the need to use air conditioning during the long summer months. Electricity may not have gone up as steeply as many other items (it does cost less in Oregon and Washington), but it isn't cheap. In some parts of the country—southern Arizona, California, and New Mexico—you will not need air conditioning at night, but your water bill will be higher. Water can be a scarce commodity in desert country, and more of it is needed there than elsewhere. Your lawn certainly requires more water. The long, hot summers will also necessitate longer use of your car's air conditioning, and that can cause an increase in fuel consumption by as much as 10 percent.

Finally, remember that there is no such thing as perfect, year-round weather.

It may seem that I've been overly negative about warm-climate areas—but I have just tried to emphasize that weather shouldn't be too important a factor in determining where to live. Retired people can stay home when it is too hot or too cold to be outdoors for a prolonged period. They can always have emergency rations on hand, and during hurricanes, for example, they can manage very well with canned foods, even when the electricity is shut off for a day or more. It is possible to make coffee and heat foods on little Sterno stoves or their equivalent.

In any case, the kind of weather that best suits

one person isn't necessarily what someone else will want. Some people, for example, prefer cold climates. Cold weather, if not too severe, is exhilarating; in fact, it offers a special interest for retirement living—the changing seasons, which are stimulating in and of themselves.

Fortunately, our country is vast and offers a broad choice. For some, living in the mountains would be best; for others, the seashore; and for still others, a desert area. While health factors are naturally important, it is also important to consider what a person finds interesting and enjoys doing. Interest and enjoyment in themselves promote good health by giving meaning to life.

You—and only you—know what extremes of temperature you can tolerate and how great an influence the weather has on your activities and your state of mind. If you plan to spend a lot of time outdoors, weather will, of course, be important to you. To obtain the official all-year weather records of a certain city, write to the National Climatic Center, Publications, Federal Building, Asheville, N.C. 28801. Ask them whether they have a "Climatological Summary" or "Local Climatological Data" on the city that interests you.

Some people have a fine solution to the problem of climate: They live in a warm-climate area during the winter and a cool one during the summer. Unfortunately, not many of us can afford to do that. But there is a less expensive way of living in two places: You can sell your furniture, give it away, or put it in storage for possible use at some future time; buy a recreational vehicle (a camper, motor home, or travel trailer); and beat the game by moving to a warm-climate area for the winter and a cool one for the summer. (See Appendix G on mobile homes and Appendix H on recreational vehicles.)

A recreational vehicle means a real vacation for your wife. It is a lot easier to take care of than an apartment or house. Your Social Security checks can be sent to your bank when you travel, and the benefits of Medicare, of course, continue in all 50 states.

Don't Decide Too Quickly

Rather than decide in advance on a certain city in a warm-climate state you may have selected for your retirement living, visit other sections of that state. You may find another city that is far more appealing to you as a place to live permanently.

You should also consider different regions of the country, rather than limiting your choices to one particular state. There may be some beautiful spots that never even occurred to you.

Unless you *must* live in a warm-climate area, don't overlook the areas around Portland, Oregon, and Seattle, Washington, where the winters are short and rarely severe. They offer a climate that is better than the one you have probably lived in most of your life. They are not the rainy areas too many believe them to be, and their rains are not the heavy ones that occur so unexpectedly in some warm-climate areas of the Southeast.

The states of Oregon and Washington have just about everything: flowers in variety and profusion, colorful deserts, great forests and rivers, and majestic snow-crowned mountains where you can walk in your shirtsleeves all summer and throw snowballs at the same time. Both states also have spectacularly scenic beaches on the Pacific Ocean.

When you retire—or before, if time permits— visit Oregon and Washington. Try to arrange an extra two or three days for visiting the beautiful cities of Vancouver and Victoria in Canada, and plan your trip so that you can also include Yellowstone National Park, Glacier National Park, and some of the other great attractions in that part of the country.

Return home by driving through California, over to Las Vegas if you wish, on to Arizona to see the Grand Canyon, and then on to New Mexico. If you are unfamiliar with that part of the country, you have a real thrill in store. If you go on to Texas, be sure to go to San Antonio and walk along the banks of the San Antonio River or take a boat ride on it.

From San Antonio, take the 230-mile drive south to McAllen, Texas. The area east and west of that city is known as the Lower Rio Grande Valley. It appeals to many people as an ideal warm-climate retirement site.

It's great to see the U.S.A. Yes, do everything possible to see all of it before you settle down permanently—anywhere.

FOREIGN COUNTRIES

Most people who want to move to another location after retiring choose a place somewhere in the United States, but there is a small number who prefer a foreign country. Many of them believe that it will cost less, but that depends, in this modern age, on where they plan to locate in the foreign country and the style in which they plan to live.

Those who prefer a warm climate such as can be found in our Southeast, South, or Southwest will, in most cases, choose Mexico, largely because of its proximity to the United States.

A man who lived in Mexico for about a year told me that those who want to live in glamorized resort cities, such as Acapulco, are going to find it expensive. In Guadalajara, where he spent most of his time, he found living expenses more reasonable.

He described it this way: "Guadalajara is Mexico's second largest city. It has a population of 1,250,-000, its altitude is a little over 5,000 feet. It has pollution-free air, a year-round temperature of 60 to 80 degrees, and a dry, mild climate that has made it popular as a health resort. It is famous for its fiestas, flowers, fountains, markets, and as the home of the strolling groups of Mexican folk musicians."

With a description like that, I was not surprised when he further informed me that more than 10,000 retired Americans live in Guadalajara and its environs.

For detailed information on Mexico, I suggest the following two books:

1. *Fabulous Mexico—Where Everything Costs Less,* by Norman D. Ford, published by Harian Publications, Greenlawn, N.Y. 11740 ($2.50).

Traveling and writing about it is Mr. Ford's specialized profession. (He is the founder of the world-famous Globe Trotters Club.) In this book he writes about Acapulco, Cuernavaca, Guadalajara, Mexico

City, Puerto Vallarta, Taxco, and some other cities. He has traveled through all of Mexico and has done extensive research to learn what the Mexican style of living offers. He gives his readers the opportunity to learn of places where life is refreshingly different, really relaxing, and comparatively inexpensive.

2. *Everything You Ever Wanted to Know About Living in Mexico,* by Norvelle Sannebeck, published by Droke House/Hallux, P.O. Box 2027, Anderson, S.C. 29621 ($4.95 plus 25¢ postage).

Mr. Sannebeck spent many years in several foreign countries while in the service of the United States diplomatic corps. Upon his retirement, he moved to Morelia, Mexico, and several years later he wrote this book. His book does an exceptional job of giving readers the facts on what they want (need) to know about living in Mexico. He explains why Mexico would be the best place for some people—but certainly not for others.

Incidentally, American automobile insurance is not valid in Mexico. It is advisable to obtain Mexican automobile insurance *before* you cross the border. (See Appendix F.)

Businessmen who make frequent trips to large cities in major foreign countries tell me that prices keep going up, a condition not unlike what we see here in our own country. Tourists who have visited a country for the second time give me the same report.

Recently a friend of mine, after his return from a second visit to Spain, informed me that although prices were higher than when he made his first trip there, they still were reasonable. He also noted an increase in the number of tourists.

Most tourists do make short visits to more than one country, and just about all of them go to the same cities, resorts, and special points of interest. Naturally prices rise in popular places, and we must realize that there will continue to be a tendency for prices to rise, by the all-too-common law of supply and demand. So it should be evident that retired people and others who want to live inexpensively—anywhere—will have to avoid those areas to which crowds of tourists are attracted.

Whether it would cost *less* to live in a foreign country than in the United States under present inflationary conditions is debatable, but the chances are that people can live *better* for the same money—at least in a material sense.

There are so many books on so many countries that I can only suggest you go to a bookstore or library to read up on the country that interests you. Encyclopedias, too, contain information on all countries, including the smallest ones.

If you move to a foreign country, your Social Security checks will be mailed to you there. You do, however, have to visit a Social Security office to fill out certain forms before you leave the United States.

Those who move to a foreign country lose the benefits of Medicare. If you have other medical insurance, check to see whether it covers you there. It may in some countries and not in others.

If you are going to move to a foreign country where English is not spoken, you will need a directory of doctors who speak English. The World Medical Association is an international federation of the most representative national medical associations of more than 60 nations of the world. Founded in 1947, it was incorporated in 1965 as a nonprofit educational and scientific organization under the laws of the state of New York. Its annual budget is dependent entirely upon dues paid by national member associations and private contributions.

To obtain a copy of their pocket-size directory listing English-speaking doctors in more than 70 foreign countries (including China) send a $2 check or money order to The World Medical Association, 10 Columbus Circle, New York, N.Y. 10019, and ask for a copy of their *International Medical Directory*.

While living costs are certainly a serious factor these days, and may be the decisive one in making a move to a country where everything *costs* less, we must realize that we may also *receive* less of the accustomed features that have made our lives pleasant, interesting, or, at the very least, bearable during our many years of living in our home country. It is difficult, if not impossible, to make a perfect decision. Everything has a price we must pay in one form or another. It is tough enough for some people to adjust to a new location in *this* country, and it may be far more difficult to do so in a foreign country.

Of course, an airplane will get you back to the United States for a visit in a matter of hours from almost any place in the world. However, the farther away the country is located, the more it will cost to do that—which is all right for those who can afford it.

Some people not only will want to move to a foreign country but will find it in their best interests to do so. Even so, they may have doubts about what their reactions will be when they live there. I therefore offer these suggestions:

1. Sell—or give away—furniture and other things that you will not need and put the rest in storage.

2. Try living in the country of your choice for several months or—for the best test—for one year. If at the end of that time you still want to stay there, have the things you left in storage shipped to you.

3. During your trial period learn the language—or at least the basics of it. It is worth learning even if you decide to return to this country.

Travel
When You Please

RETIREMENT offers new opportunities, and new opportunities can make a new life. Your new life will be interesting and enjoyable if you make the most of all the special advantages you have now. This is the time to travel, because there's no one to tell you when you must go or when you must return. It's your first real chance to travel without having to watch the calendar. You have complete freedom to adjust your trips according to the season of the year, which makes it possible to choose particular places when their climate is most favorable.

If you travel by car, you can take your time and avoid the rush hours and busy holiday traffic. You can drive leisurely and make travel by car the relaxation it should be. There are some other special advantages:

You make your own schedule. If you feel like

sleeping late, or if you aren't feeling tip-top, or if you are having such a good time that you want to stay on, you can delay your departure from a stop you have made without risk of missing a train or plane. You can change your plans without worrying about whether you are losing excursion rates or whether a couple of extra days force you to add a whole week to wait for transportation.

If something catches your eye along the road, you can detour for as short or as long a time as you choose. Most seasoned travelers will tell you that the unexpected surprises are the ones you remember the longest —but you have to make it possible for them to happen.

Millions now travel in campers, motor homes, or travel trailers. It is a low-cost way to see the country, and it is also a good investment. When they are no longer needed for travel, they can be lived in permanently, sold, or parked in some country place and used as a second home for weekends or vacations. For further comment and information on campers, motor homes, and travel trailers, refer to Appendix H.

You may want to write beforehand to see which parks have facilities for camping and recreational vehicles. Addresses of the national parks are given in Appendix D.

Of course there are some disadvantages to motor traveling: mechanical trouble, poor roads and detours, bad driving weather. You can try to avoid these problems by good planning (see the section on driving tips), but you can't have a guarantee. And so, if you decide against this method of traveling, try the trains (which are improving now), buses, planes, or any number of combinations, including car rentals.

If you have never taken an airplane trip, do so. It is truly a great experience. Once you travel that way, you probably will want to do it always, especially for long distances.

If you're not too sure about bus traveling, try a short trip to find out whether you like it. Traveling by bus offers many excellent advantages, but it is restricting in that you can't move around as you can in a plane or on a train, and you can't stop and get out as you can when traveling in your own car. But the seats are very comfortable and adjustable, the coaches are air conditioned, and long-distance buses are equipped with bathroom facilities.

Bus companies sell special passes for unlimited travel within a specified time period, which makes it very inexpensive if you expect to move around a lot. Write to any one of the interstate bus companies, such as Greyhound or Trailways, for their pamphlets on tours and special tips for traveling by bus. They can give you many ideas and suggestions.

Perhaps you are not interested in long-distance traveling. Then take a short vacation now and then and go to a different place each time. Visit nearby cities and places you found interesting and enjoyable on previous trips. Now that you don't have to watch the calendar, spend enough of the time you now have to really see and enjoy them. If you have moved to another location, take a trip back to your former hometown once in a while to visit relatives and old friends.

Several short vacations are often better than a single, long one. A city 25 miles away might do you as much good as a trip to Europe. Change, not the place, is the point of traveling.

All right, you are almost convinced to take that trip. But you still have a few doubts and worries in the back of your mind.

Worried about your Social Security checks? Forget it. They can be sent to your bank. All you have to do is arrange for a change of address, and have the checks sent to you in care of your bank. Use Treasury Form 233, available at most banks, to grant power of attorney to your bank, authorizing the deposit of your check to either your checking or savings account.

Don't worry about Medicare. Chances are that you will feel so good you will not need medical attention. But to put your mind at ease, the benefits of Medicare, and your eligibility, continue in all 50 states. Or perhaps you have a medical problem such that you fear traveling too far afield. Medic Alert takes care of such conditions. In an emergency, collect telephone calls can be made from any part of the world for detailed data about the patient, 24 hours a day, every day. For additional information, write to Medic Alert Foundation International, Turlock, Calif. 95380.

Don't worry about your mail piling up on your front stoop. The post office will hold mail up to 30 days, provided you make the request in writing. Make other arrangements if you plan to be gone for a longer period.

Your pets can travel with you. A 54-page directory of motels and hotels in the United States and Canada that accept guests with pets can be obtained by sending a check or money order for 50 cents to GAINES, P.O. Box 1007, Kankakee, Ill. 60901. The directory is called *Touring with Towser*.

Perhaps your most serious objection to travel is

that you have a limited income. Low-priced motels are found away from the expressways, in town or just outside. They may not have a swimming pool, TV, a bar, or a restaurant, but they are clean and inexpensive. Since the increase in development and popularity of first-class motels, many hotels have reduced their rates and offer free parking as well. You lose the advantage of having fairly private outdoor lounging space, but if your stay is to be short, it may not matter.

Budget motels are now established across the country. Appendix E contains a partial list of chains that charge comparatively low rates. To find out where these chains have motels, what they offer, and what their rates are, write to them for their directories. A collection of directories would give you fairly good coverage of the United States.

Private houses with guest rooms can be found in all parts of the country. Their rates are invariably lower than those of commercial hotels or motels, and some serve breakfast, usually at an additional cost. They are clean and very pleasant. If you know when you will arrive in a certain town, you can reserve space ahead of time. Lists of guest houses are available from the local chamber of commerce and state tourist offices.

Restaurants that are located away from the expressways are apt to serve better food, and to have lower prices, because they depend on local, repeat customers rather than tourists. Good food—and plenty of it—can generally be had where truckers eat. Watch for restaurants where a lot of trucks are parked, especially at mealtimes.

Here is a lead to getting good food at fair prices: As you approach a city (off the expressways) watch for an emblem or sign showing where the Kiwanis, Lions, Rotary, and other clubs meet for lunch. Since the members of such clubs live in that city, they know where the good food is.

As a general rule, cafeterias offer a large and varied assortment of good food at reasonable prices. You see the food, which helps to make a choice. They also offer many kinds of salads, which are good for you, especially when driving long distances. The coffee shop of a hotel is usually another good place to eat.

A final word about restaurants: A high price does not guarantee a good meal, and a low price does not indicate a bad one. For the most part you will have to take your chances. Even if you want to treat yourself to the best meal in town, you must take the word of someone who has eaten there.

TRAVEL—WHERE?

Let's say you have decided on a trip. If you are an experienced traveler, you already know what sorts of places attract you the most. You know what you want to go back to see again, or you have certain places in mind that you have long wanted to visit. Now is your chance, and you only have to decide when, how, and for how long.

But if you have never been much of a traveler, you may be confused by the endless choices and possibilities. Instead of making an impulsive decision, think about what you would really enjoy the most. Perhaps you've always lived in a large city and never had the chance to spend time in the country. Or maybe you've never seen a desert. Our country is so varied that you can visit almost any kind of scenic area without having to travel great distances.

If you haven't traveled much, my advice is to see the U.S.A. first. You will not need a passport. You won't have to get your photograph taken, and you won't need shots against cholera, smallpox, typhoid, or yellow fever. There will be no need to carry an English/foreign language dictionary, because everyone will understand you and you will understand them. You will be familiar with what you are eating and drinking.

You will know how much you are paying for everything. You won't have to burden your brain to figure out money exchange, and you won't have to decipher restaurant menus and bills or feel frustrated by not knowing how much to tip.

My purpose here is to whet your appetite. Most people are aware of the obvious points of interest, but simply don't know how much else there is to see. People generally know their own state; Kentuckians know, for example, that there is a lot more to Kentucky than Louisville and Mammoth Cave. You have not seen Maine if you only visit Portland, and you certainly don't know California if you only visit San Francisco and Yosemite.

If the wonders of nature are at the top of your list, first look into the national parks. You are wrong if you think you have to go West to see them. In addition to the well-known wonders of the world—Grand Canyon, Yellowstone, Yosemite, Sequoia—consider the Everglades in Florida, Platt in Oklahoma, Shenandoah in Virginia, Acadia in Maine. Appendix D has a complete list of all national parks in the United States and their addresses. Write for details, including possible times of the year when the parks may be closed because of weather conditions. Select the addresses in the area that interests you.

Don't neglect the mountains of New England (which are very different from the great mountain ranges of the West), the rolling hills of Pennsylvania, the Adirondack lakes of New York, the bayous of Louisiana, Big Sur in California, the Badlands of Dakota. Don't forget the St. Lawrence Seaway in Upstate New York and Canada and the lake areas of Wisconsin, Michigan, and Minnesota.

You don't have to be a Tom Sawyer and travel the Mississippi River on a raft, but you can travel that same river on an old stern-wheeler riverboat. Like Tom Sawyer, play hooky and take that trip on the *Delta Queen* riverboat. (For information write to Greene Line Steamers, Inc., 322 East 4th Street, Cincinnati, Ohio 45202.)

If history excites your imagination, again you can find things of interest in almost any area. Our earliest history extends well beyond the New England settlers and the scenes of the American Revolution. The Spanish left their mark in the Southwest (see the missions in California and the oldest church in Santa Fe) and in Florida, where you can visit the oldest city in the United States, St. Augustine. See the battlefield at Gettysburg, visit the Alamo. There are places of historical value in every state, and state travel bureaus are happy to send you literature about them.

Sturbridge Village in Massachusetts, Knott's Berry Farm in California, and Williamsburg in Virginia recreate our past as it was a couple of hundred years ago. You can see the life of the Indians as it was —in Mesa Verde, for example—and as it is today in the pueblos of New Mexico. Get a bit of the flavor of the Old West in the ghost towns of Arizona and Nevada; visit the ranch country of today's West in Wyoming or Texas. See the Pennsylvania Dutch country, see Las Vegas, see the Mardi Gras in New Orleans, see San Francisco. See how the rich lived (visit William Randolph Hearst's villa at San Simeon, California, lifted stone by stone from Europe and reassembled) and see how the famous lived (go to Jefferson's home in Monticello, Virginia). And above all, see New York, which has so many attractions that it is discussed in a separate section of this chapter.

Like to see how things are done? Catch a county fair to watch animals judged, tour a newspaper plant, a winery, a Hollywood film studio, the Chicago stockyards, the Houston Space Center, a shipyard. See the canal locks in Sault Ste. Marie, Michigan, or the old, now unused Erie Canal in New York. Take a tour of the Grand Coulee Dam in Washington or Hoover Dam between Arizona and Nevada.

For fun, see Disneyland near Los Angeles—a must for children and a real tonic for older people. If you're in Florida, see Disney World near Orlando. The Denver and Rio Grande Western Railroad has a narrow-gauge line between Durango and Silverton in Colorado, a distance of about 45 miles. You can make it in one day, with a stopover for lunch at Silverton.

By all means, visit Washington, D.C. There is so much to see there that you should get all the information you can well in advance so that you can plan your time. Write to: Washington Convention & Visitors Bureau, 1129 20th Street, N.W., Washington, D.C. 20036.

There is a new visitors' center in Washington called Ralph Nader's Public Citizen Visitors Center. The address is 1200 15th Street, N.W., Washington, D.C. 20005. It's open all day during the week as well as until 1 P.M. on Sundays. The group's position is that there is more to see in Washington than monuments, that a tourist to the capital should become issue-oriented, conscious of his rights and duties as a citizen. The agency arranges for tourists to observe government hearings, meet congressmen, and get a look at some of the special-interest groups that have headquarters in Washington.

No matter what area or city you have in mind, find out in advance what the weather conditions are likely to be at the time of your trip. Also get information about trade fairs, sporting events, and drama and music festivals that may be scheduled. The best source for local information is the chamber of commerce. You can get addresses from telephone directories of other cities at your own local telephone company office. Write also to the U.S. Travel Service of the Department of Commerce, 14th Street, N.W., Washington, D.C. 20230, which especially promotes travel in the United States. You would do well to write to as many sources as possible so that once you have chosen where to go, you can be sure to cover all the points of interest.

Keep in mind that our bicentennial celebration will fall in 1976. Plans are being made to mark the year in all parts of the country, so try to take advantage of the special events.

If you decide to travel outside the United States, get the advice and practical help of a travel agency. Its people can answer just about any question you may have. They will make reservations for you, including car rental, and you will avoid language difficulties in trying to make those arrangements yourself.

Be sure to find out about requirements for passport, visas, and inoculations. Again, your travel agent will be able to give you all the necessary information, and will even take care of some of the details.

Be sure to read up on what to see. There are any number of excellent travel books to help you plan your itinerary carefully so that you can line up your reservations in advance.

If you have never traveled abroad before, you might want to try a cruise that makes a number of stops. Cruises range from short ones of three or four days to long ones of several months. There are many advantages for older people who don't want the wear and tear of packing and unpacking and getting from place to place. Your ship is your hotel for the entire trip. You can pick and choose your dates, your stopovers, the length of time you will be away, and even the kind of food you eat. (You can have Italian food on an Italian ship, smorgasbord on a Swedish liner, or American food on an American ship.) Most cruises leave from New York City, but many originate in Florida. And, of course, the West Coast has trips to the Pacific and the Panama Canal Zone.

If you have a real spirit of adventure, investigate a trip on a freighter. The accommodations are far from luxurious, but the food is simple and good. Many freighters stop at ports that are off the beaten track.

Above all, they are quite inexpensive. Nowadays most of them carry a medical staff. Know that in bad weather the going can be pretty rough. Harian Publications (Greenlawn, N.Y. 11740) puts out three paperbacks on the subject: *Travel Routes Around the World* ($1.50); *Today's Outstanding Buys in Freighter Travel* ($3.95); *Freighter Days* ($2.50).

New York City

New York City is the greatest show on earth. If you exclude peace and quiet and orderliness, New York has more and better of just about anything you can name. It may also have the worst of a lot of things, but all in all, people who know it well think it is the most exciting and stimulating city in the world. And in many ways it is very beautiful.

People? There are one million visitors in New York every single day of the year, both as tourists and on business. Every working day, more than two million people converge on Lower Manhattan to fill the office buildings in the area from the southern tip of the island to 59th Street at the foot of Central Park.

New Yorkers live in Little Italy and Chinatown (both in Lower Manhattan); there are large settlements of German-Americans in Yorkville (in the 80s on the East Side); Puerto Ricans in East Harlem and the Lower East Side; Middle Easterners in and around Atlantic Avenue in Brooklyn. Just about every nationality you can name lays claim to a specific area throughout the five boroughs. Each of these neighborhoods has restaurants, grocery stores, and shops that offer food, clothing, and household items from the mother country. If you have a longing to hear the sound of the lan-

guage your parents spoke, by all means walk through
the streets of that part of the city where recent settlers
and their families live.

Cultural activities? New York's museums are
among the world's greatest and most varied. Lincoln
Center is a handsome complex of buildings where
opera, ballet, theater, and symphonic and chamber music are presented every week of the year. Broadway is
still the heart of the country's theater, and many excellent shows are given in other parts of the city as well.
In the summer, free open-air concerts are given in
parks of each of the five boroughs, and plays are
presented almost every night in a beautiful outdoor
theater in Central Park at no charge to the public.

For architectural achievements, naturally everyone will want to visit the very modern Whitney and
Guggenheim museums, the Seagram Building, and the
Plaza Hotel. But don't overlook the Cathedral of St.
John the Divine, the largest Gothic cathedral in the
world and still incomplete, or Temple Emanu-El, the
largest synagogue of modern times, with its Roman-
esque and Byzantine and Near Eastern design elements.
For late-nineteenth-century homes, visit the row houses
designed by McKim, Mead, and White in Harlem's St.
Nicholas Historic District. To go way back, visit the
Cloisters, a branch of the Metropolitan Museum. Its
medieval monasteries and chapels were brought from
Europe and rebuilt stone by stone.

Spectator sports? Shea Stadium in Queens is the
home of the Jets for the football season and the Mets
and Yankees for the baseball season. The new Madison
Square Garden features hockey and basketball in season, and presents other special events, including track

meets, boxing, wrestling, and tennis. Several racetracks are in the area, including harness racing.

The Coliseum, the nation's leading exposition center, holds automobile shows, antique shows, dog shows, flower shows, wine-tasting festivals, and special trade shows.

Don't plan to use your car in the city. You can get anywhere by bus or subway, and taxis are plentiful except at rush hours—8:30 to 9:30 A.M. and 4:30 to 5:30 P.M.—and in the early evening hours before theater time.

There are many ways to see New York. You can sightsee by helicopter or tour bus. You can take a boat ride around Manhattan Island. For 5 cents, a ferryboat ride to Staten Island will give you a good look at the Verrazano-Narrows Bridge, the world's longest suspension span. Take the boat to the Statue of Liberty. You can climb the stairs inside the statue for a spectacular view of Lower Manhattan or the ocean beyond or just leisurely stroll along the grounds of Liberty Island, perhaps stopping in at New York's newest museum, which traces the story of the city's immigrants.

The city bus system has two "Culture Loop" tours, which make specified stops. For $1 you can get on or off at any of these stops with a ticket that is good for the best part of the day (10 A.M. to 6 P.M.). Buses run every 15 minutes.

A delightful ride is through Central Park in a hansom cab pulled by a flower-decked horse. Your driver might be a portly man wearing a stovepipe hat or a long-haired young girl wearing dungarees.

Last, but not least, *walk*. Put on your most comfortable shoes and just *go*—up and down famous Fifth

Avenue, both the shopping district and the uptown, handsome residential part facing Central Park; Park Avenue, with a beautifully planted center strip that runs almost its entire length. Take the subway or bus downtown and walk through Battery Park at the tip of the island and the financial district. In fact, take two trips to Wall Street: one during the day to experience the bustle and excitement, and then on the weekend or a holiday, when the area is almost ghostly.

There has been extensive new construction in this area, with some of Manhattan's finest sights, especially One Chase Manhattan Plaza and the twin skyscrapers of the new World Trade Center, which tops the famous Empire State Building. And, of course, two old favorite visiting places are here: Trinity Church and its cemetery, and the Treasury Building.

Incidentally, the Parks Department and one of the city museums conduct walking tours through different parts of the city, usually on Sundays from spring through fall. Keep your eyes open for outdoor sculpture by some of the world's greats: Henry Moore and Alexander Calder (Lincoln Center), Pablo Picasso (Greenwich Village), Jean Dubuffet (Chase Manhattan Plaza).

You will also enjoy a visit to Brooklyn Heights, a part of the city that has kept the look of old New York. You can take a short subway or taxi ride there or you can do what so many New Yorkers do—walk across the Brooklyn Bridge. While there, go to the promenade along Columbia Heights for one of the very best views of Manhattan as well as of the harbor activity—tugboats, tankers, liners, all coming and going in the East River and the Narrows.

Another excellent view of the city, of course, is from the top of the Empire State Building. But also try the Gulf + Western Building at Columbus Circle or the RCA Building in Rockefeller Center or the "Top of the Sixes" on Fifth Avenue. Have a cocktail or an early dinner at one of these rooftop restaurants; the city is at its best just when the lights are going on.

If you are in New York when the weather is mild, don't miss a walk in Central Park on a Sunday. New Yorkers really use their parks, and you will see steel bands, storytellers, guitar-playing folksingers, ball-games, model sailboats, perhaps a karate or pantomime demonstration, and hundreds of people cycling and walking (cars are banned on weekends). Central Park has a delightful children's zoo as well as a small regular zoo.

If you really like zoos, don't miss the Bronx Zoo, one of the world's greatest. Two of its main attractions are its World of Darkness exhibition, featuring noctural animals, and the African Plains, where only a moat separates the animals and the spectators.

Both the Bronx and Brooklyn have famous botanical gardens. Brooklyn's has three Japanese gardens and a world-famous bonsai collection. In the spring its walk of flowering cherry trees rivals that of Washington, D.C.

There is just no room to list all the "must-sees" in New York. Even people who have never been to New York know about Greenwich Village, Coney Island, the United Nations, the Rockettes at Radio City Music Hall, Times Square, and the fact that New York has the best restaurants in the country. Whatever you want to know, you can find out at the New York

Convention and Visitors Bureau, 90 East 42nd Street, New York, N.Y. 10017, directly opposite Grand Central Station. You can get free literature, guidebooks and maps, lists of hotels and restaurants and shops, a seasonal calendar of events, special services, tickets to TV shows. Just about any question you may have can be answered there. Write to the Bureau in advance so that you can plan your time well and make reservations. The staff is international.

PACKING SUGGESTIONS

A most important tip: Don't lock your bags until the very last minute; you are sure to find something that must either go in or come out. Have a carryall or large shopping bag to hold last-minute items or to carry those things you may be glad to have handy at a moment's notice.

Travel clock. Even if the clock is in its own case, take along an empty box into which the case fits. Leave the empty box in your baggage to remind you to pack the clock when you are ready to leave your hotel. Travel clocks are easily forgotten, especially when you're in a hurry.

Pajamas, shirts. Take colored pajamas and shirts, not white ones. Colors are seen more readily against a white sheet, so they are less likely to be overlooked when you are packing.

Slippers. Put a cloth bag in your luggage. It will remind you to pack those slippers, which may be hiding under the bed. A cloth bag for extra shoes will keep them from soiling your clothes. Shoes and slippers should have air, so unless they are wet, don't use plastic bags for them.

For a list of specific items that you may forget or simply not think about—and then just may want on your trip—see the accompanying chart.

MISCELLANEOUS TIPS

Baggage. When checking into a motel, hotel, airport, railroad station, or any other place, don't set your baggage down where someone might fall over it. You could become involved in a lawsuit.

Tag all baggage. If a suitcase is lost, left behind, or picked up in error, you will have a better and quicker chance of recovering it. Your name and address not only should be attached to the outside of each bag; it should also be placed inside each bag for identification in case the outside tag is ripped off. Keeping a description of your baggage (exact measurements, colors, special trim) also helps to identify it much faster.

If you travel by airplane, you might be interested in knowing that Eastern Airlines operates a baggage tracing system in Charlotte, North Carolina, which serves most of the world's airlines. If a bag does not have a name and address tag on the outside, the personnel open the bag to try to find identification inside. They are able to open luggage without damaging it.

The Air Transport Association advises the removal of all obsolete destination tags to help prevent bags from being delivered to the wrong place.

THINGS TO TAKE ALONG

Eyeglasses. Take a spare pair, or your prescription. Losing or breaking your glasses can spoil your trip.

Knife. A small, sharp knife (a pocketknife will do) and a screwdriver will come in handy.

Collapsible cup and heating coil. Clean, convenient drinking glasses aren't always available. And you may feel like having an early morning cup of coffee, or a cup of hot soup when you don't want to go out.

Notebook or pad of paper. Keep addresses and notes handy. In fact, make notes of what you want to ask or tell people you visit. It's so easy to forget in the excitement of visiting people you haven't seen for a long time.

Pen. Just when you need one, you'll have to look around for it.

Plastic bags. Very useful for packing damp laundry, for separating soiled clothing from clean, and for packing shoes, particularly dirty ones. Large plastic bags, big enough to slip over your shoes, make an excellent protection for your feet in heavy rains. Take along some rubber bands, or cord, that you can use to fasten them above your ankles. (Note: Do not fit the rubber band or cord too tight; it can cause your ankles to swell.)

Medication. Whether it's something you use regularly or in emergencies, have enough with you so that you don't need to visit a doctor for a special prescription. As a precaution take along something to treat diarrhea, overeating, or overdrinking; even the water in some regions may upset your digestion.

Inflatable pillow. You may not like the one you get to sleep on. In addition, it's useful in the car, for either the driver to put behind his back or the passenger to rest his head against. Cover it in a colored fabric.

Electric pad or hot water bottle.

Tissues, premoisturized towelettes (such as Wash 'N Dri), and paper towels. Take plenty along. They are good for wiping the windshield, freshening up after an impromptu roadside picnic, wiping shoes, and so on.

Survival kit. If you expect to be away from towns for any length of time, such a kit comes in handy. It should include eating utensils, a flare, some simple tools, and so on.

First-aid kit.

Don't leave baggage exposed—or even visible—in a car unless you can watch it. Don't put anything of value in the glove compartment, even if you lock it. Thieves can easily break into it, looking for cameras and other small valuables.

English-speaking doctors in foreign countries. If you are going on a trip to a foreign country you should know how to reach a doctor who speaks English. I again recommend the *International Medical Directory,* which lists English-speaking doctors in more than 70 foreign countries, including China, and costs $2. Write to The World Medical Association, 10 Columbus Circle, New York, N.Y. 10019.

A free directory is available from the International Association for Medical Assistance to Travelers, a division of the Foundation for International Medical Training. Write to the Association about the advantages of its membership card. The address is 350 Fifth Avenue, New York, N.Y. 10001.

Golden Age and Golden Eagle Passports. People 62 years of age or older can obtain, without charge, a Golden Age Passport. Those under 62 years of age can obtain a Golden Eagle Passport for $10. Both passports are valid for the entire year in which they are issued. They admit the holder and all other passengers traveling with the holder in a single, noncommercial vehicle to unlimited free admission to our national parks or other federal recreation areas where entrance fees are charged. They are obtainable only at those places.

Holders of these passports are not granted prior rights when the facilities at the park or other recreation area are filled to capacity. All these facilities are run on a first-come, first-serve basis, which is the fair way.

Where fees are charged for use of certain facilities, such as campgrounds, the holders of Golden Age Passports will be allowed a 50 percent discount. This does not apply where a facility is operated by a concessionaire.
Holidays (*just a memo*). There are now five three-day holiday weekends each year when the traffic is extra heavy. Since you are now able to arrange your own time, keep this in mind when planning a trip. These days have been legally set aside as national holidays:

Washington's Birthday: Third Monday in February
Memorial Day: Last Monday in May
Labor Day: First Monday in September
Columbus Day: Second Monday in October
Veterans Day: Fourth Monday in October

Ice (*saving it*). If you take ice or have it delivered to your room, wrapping the container in newspaper will keep it from melting for a long time, even overnight.
Homemade litter basket. A large paper bag can be made into a handy litter basket by folding the entire top outward an inch or more and then pressing the folded part. If you want it square in shape, pinch each corner.

DRIVING TIPS

Now that you are retired, chances are you will be using your car often to go on trips. This section is intended for those retired people who did not have the time to do much driving before their retirement, not for those who are experienced drivers and, accordingly, know the tips listed here.

These tips are based on personal experience in driving more than 1,250,000 accident-free miles, in all kinds of weather, during my 41 years as a traveling salesman.

Before you go. The cost of joining AAA or a similar organization is well worthwhile. Even aside from the useful information they can provide, should you get into trouble on the road and need towing or special service, there are local affiliates everywhere. You can get current information on roads, weather, and motels as well as fees, group tours, and other special points of interest.

Be sure you have adequate insurance and up-to-date licenses; check with your doctor to make sure your vision and reflexes are in A-1 condition.

Your car. Have a mechanic check your car before you leave to make sure these items are in perfect working order: windshield wiper, lights and signals, tires. Keep the windshield clean to avoid eyestrain, and use sunglasses in bright sunlight or in snow-covered country. It's a good idea to check your fan belt too. When driving long distances, have the tire pressure and water in the radiator checked every day.

On the Road

When traveling for pleasure, try to schedule your driving so that you can avoid the highways and town roads that are heavily trafficked at rush hours.

Keep a road atlas in the car. You may know how to get to your friend's home, but an unexpected detour could really disorient you.

Expenses can be controlled in many small ways. For example, gasoline taxes vary from state to state, with a low of 9 cents per gallon in Texas to a high of 14 cents in Connecticut. Exxon puts out an excellent little booklet called *Touring Tips,* which lists the tax in every state. To get a copy, write to: Exxon Touring Service, 1251 Avenue of the Americas, New York, N.Y. 10020. Often you can save by filling up in a low-tax state before passing into a high-tax one. And if you know in advance which roads have tolls, you can usually find an alternate road. It may take a little longer to reach your destination, but it may also be a more scenic route.

When not to drive. Don't drive a car if you are very angry. Stop and get out of the car and walk five miles, if you need that much time to cool off. You may save your life, that of your passenger, and possibly the lives of other drivers and passengers.

Don't drive when you are sleepy. When you are tired, park in a safe place and take a rest or a catnap. A big meal can cause drowsiness, so when on a long drive eat several small meals rather than one large one. It breaks up the trip and you are less likely to overeat.

Don't drive after more than one drink or when you are taking medication that may affect your alertness or your reflexes.

Don't drive when the weather is really bad.

Keys. To avoid locking yourself out of your car, have two extra ignition keys made. Your wife should carry one and you should attach the other to your household key ring. Don't attach it to some secret place outside the car. It may fall off or you may forget where you hid it; besides, thieves know all the hiding places.

When parking in an attended parking lot, carry the trunk key on your household key ring, too.

The steering wheel. The only way to control a car properly under any and all conditions is to keep *both* hands on the steering wheel.

Time out. On a long trip, get out of the car periodically and walk, stretch, or do any other form of exercise; do it for mental and physical relief—and for safety. Keep a thermos of hot coffee or tea in the car for a coffee break.

Turn signals. Do not depend entirely on the other driver's turn signals. Some drivers turn them on too soon; others forget to turn them off. At the same time, you should always use yours to let other drivers know your intentions.

Left turns. It is sometimes safer, and often time-saving, to go around a few blocks than to make a left turn. Furthermore, statistics prove that more pedestrians are hit by cars making left turns than by those making right turns.

Children. Try to stay clear of cars carrying children, especially if any of them are up front with the driver. The more children, the greater the danger. Your grandchildren, of course, are well behaved in a car, but you have no way of knowing about other children in other cars. The same applies to the other driver's dog if that dog is lively and is permitted to jump around in the car. Naturally you should be sure that there are no distractions in your car.

Mountain driving. Contrary to the belief of many, mountain driving is safer than driving on some other highways. Of course, if a person wants to commit suicide, speeding on a mountain highway is an easy way

to accomplish it. Use low gear when going downhill;
otherwise your brake linings will burn out.

If you are not used to altitudes above 7,000 feet,
consult your doctor before planning your trip.

Railroad crossings. To avoid knocking your front
end out of alignment and for a less bumpy ride (as well
as for safety) come to a full stop before crossing railroad tracks or any other rough, hard surface. Proceed
slowly, allowing some free play in the steering wheel.

An aside. Now for a different kind of warning. It
may not apply to you, but if it does it may be the most
important bit of advice I can give you.

Some wives, when they are sitting beside their
husband in a car, use the occasion to criticize him.
And some men think there is no such thing as a good
woman driver. Don't choose this time to deflate the
other person's ego. A driver needs to be relaxed but
alert; trying to fend off insults can lead to tension and
annoyance that can result in an accident. (Some men
are so stubborn that it might be better to let them get
lost than to make them angry.)

If one of you really doesn't trust the other's driving don't take a car trip together. Even if you keep
quiet, your uneasiness or fear will come through and
there will no pleasure in the trip.

If you are interested in advice from professional
truck drivers, write for a free, 24-page booklet called
Practical Driving Tips. It is put out by the Public Rela-
tions Department of the American Trucking Associations, Inc., 1616 P Street, N.W., Washington, D.C.
20036.

Put Yourself to Work

REMEMBER, retirement does not have to mean idleness or boredom. Being active enhances the precious time that is now yours to use as you wish. Perhaps a hobby or traveling is not for you; then consider the possibilities of a job. A job will keep you active and enable you to meet and mix with other people. Also, it presents you with challenges that keep your mind keen and up to date.

Once you have decided that you want a job, you should give some thought to just how far you want to commit yourself, not only in time and energy but in attention as well. Don't take a full-time job if you know that you need to rest part of each day, or that you will want to be free to come and go as you please. Don't take a volunteer job that involves working with people if you aren't prepared to follow through; when people come to depend on you, it is unfair to disappoint them.

If money is a big consideration, naturally you will feel you must overlook other things. But a word of caution: Don't make the mistake of trying to fool yourself and your employer that you are capable of more than you can actually deliver.

There are endless opportunities for work. Here, we classify work into three general categories—commercial, government, and volunteer—and each will be discussed in turn.

COMMERCIAL EMPLOYMENT

Perhaps your first approach should be to your former employer. If he valued your work before, he will still value it. If he has no job for you, perhaps he will recommend you to some other company that can use your experience. Some companies will employ a retired man if he releases them from all benefits or pensions that regular employees receive.

Temporary, Part-time, and Full-time Jobs

Temporary jobs have some advantages. You can choose the work you find most interesting, and you can usually choose your hours to suit your convenience. If you can prove that you are dependable and that you are a good worker, it may lead to a permanent job.

There are many ways to find temporary jobs. Your local chamber of commerce can sometimes help you. Look in the Yellow Pages of your telephone book under the heading "Temporary Help Contractors" or

"Employment Contractors, Temporary Help." Most contractors pay your salary directly, not the company they send you to work for.

Mature Temps is an employment service that specializes in securing temporary jobs for older people and for people of all ages with mature work attitudes. They do not charge a fee. There are branch offices in major cities throughout the country. A list of their addresses follows:

THE EAST

120 Boylston Street
Boston, Mass. 02116

1114 Avenue of the Americas
New York, N.Y. 10036

1700 Market Street
Philadelphia, Pa. 19103

1 Plymouth Meeting Mall
Plymouth Meeting, Pa. 19462

East Orange, N.J.
Call for appointment:
201-672-8700

1750 K Street, N.W.
Washington, D.C. 20006

10 East Baltimore Street
Baltimore, Md. 21202

THE WEST

3727 West 6th Street
Los Angeles, Calif. 90020

11 Third Street
Hearst Building
San Francisco, Calif. 94103

THE SOUTHEAST

230 Peachtree Street, N.W.
Atlanta, Ga. 30303

THE MIDWEST

17 North State Street
Chicago, Ill. 60602

One Main Place
Dallas, Texas 75250

Full discussion of finding a job is not within the scope of this book, but it might be worthwhile to list a few kinds of part-time jobs just in case you have never given any thought to it and aren't aware of what they are: restaurant cashier; ticket seller at movie houses, theaters, and the like; salesman in retail stores; clerical

worker in an office or library; typist; driver; bank teller.
Generally these jobs are not difficult, and require only
a few hours each day. However, you do have to be
there at set hours.

You can apply to commercial employment agencies, approach people you know, or inquire at your
local chamber of commerce for suggestions. But be
sure also to go to the state employment office in your
area. These offices exist to serve everyone without cost
or obligation. Their specialists can provide counseling,
and they then try to match applicants with jobs for
which they are qualified—or lead them to training if
necessary. In addition, if the office does not have actual
listings of job openings under the state civil service
system, it can refer applicants to the proper state office
from which they can obtain information.

Jobs to Be Done at Home

There are many opportunities for earning extra income
by working at home, but be sure that the people you
deal with are thoroughly reliable so that you can depend on being properly paid for what you do. A number of companies rely on independent homeworkers to
make or assemble their product, but some of them have
been exposed as frauds.

The Homeworkers Manual is a 44-page guide-
book with comments on misleading advertisers. It also
includes the names of nonprofit organizations that offer
free advice as well as free booklets about work that can
be done at home for pay. To obtain a copy of the guide-
book, send a check or money order for $2 to Max
Cantos, P.O. Box 423, North Miami, Fla. 33160.

Salesman for Outside Calls

Many companies have a steady need for good salesmen and are well disposed to hiring older men if only because they can be pretty sure that a man past retirement age is not likely to become a competitor.

Some salesmen work on a basic salary, others on commission. Get started by calling on a local manufacturer or wholesaler and see if you can represent him in your area.

There are many product lines you can consider. Here are a few suggestions: lightweight clothing, food specialties, jewelry, handbags or wallets, lightweight sporting goods items, tourist souvenirs or postcards. Others are hardware, plumbing supplies, or toys that can be shown from a catalog or with lightweight samples.

Don't worry if you don't know anything about the product. If you are willing to learn, the retail dealers will cooperate and help you.

Offer to work on commission. A commission man is seldom refused by any company because the employer knows the salesman will have to be on his toes to earn any money. To clinch the job, say that you do not want a commission on any orders until after you have personally obtained your first one from their present customers.

Some companies give their salaried and commissioned salesmen an allowance for using their own cars to conduct company business; others furnish transportation. If you do use your own car and no allowance is given by the company, you are entitled to an income tax deduction.

Don't become discouraged when you fail to get

any orders in one day, two days, or even more. It does happen. If you carry a line of proper quality at fair prices, and if you represent a company that gives good service, you will obtain your share of orders.

Starting Your Own Business

Starting your own business entails a risk. According to statistics, any new business has only a 50 percent chance of surviving beyond two or three years. The majority of business failures are the result of one basic problem—lack of proper management.

If you have had experience as a business manager, it will certainly be a definite advantage in a business venture. But if you have not had that experience and don't want to incur the expense of hiring someone, you will find the services of SCORE very helpful.

Launched by the Small Business Administration in 1964, SCORE is the Service Corps of Retired Executives. SCORE counselors are men and women who have successfully completed their own active business careers and offer their services—without pay—to help people in small businesses with operating problems. Each has operated his own business or has specialized in some field of business activity, such as accounting, advertising, finance, or management. If, in working with you, a SCORE counselor encounters a problem in which he has not had any experience, he will call in another SCORE counselor with that experience to help.

You can get in touch with SCORE by visiting or writing to the field office of the Small Business Administration in your city or the one nearest to it. For a complete list of the field offices, refer to Appendix B.

To go into a business of your own, you will need

a license. If you want to operate from your home, check to see what the restrictions are or if there is an ordinance against it.

The following publications will be useful:

Small Business Marketers Aids No. 71. Check List for Going into Business. A free copy can be obtained from the Small Business Administration's office in or near your city.

Starting and Managing a Small Business of Your Own—SBA-1.15:1. Send a check or money order for 35 cents to Superintendent of Documents, U.S. Government Printing Office, Washington, D.C. 20402.

Owning Your Own Business. This is a cassette produced by David D. Seltz and can be obtained by mailing a check or money order for $10 payable to him at 240 Madison Avenue, New York, N.Y. 10016. It gives valuable information for selecting a business opportunity, whether franchised or nonfranchised. Accompanying it is a Self-Scoring Check List that helps a person know whether he is suited for the kind of business he has decided on.

How to Start a Profitable Retirement Business, by Arthur Liebers. Send a check or money order for $2 to Pilot Books, Inc., 347 Fifth Avenue, New York, N.Y. 10016. This book suggests many kinds of businesses a person can start on his own and gives complete information about them. It is only 56 pages, but its contents more than make up for its size.

I have two suggestions for a part-time business of your own. I recommend them because they entail no overhead, they can be operated from the home, the cash investment is small, and all expenses are tax deductible.

Baby-sitting. If you enjoy children and have the patience to deal with them, you can operate a baby-sitting service. Both you and your wife can do it, separately or together. Instead of sitting in your own home reading or watching television, why not do that while baby-sitting and get paid for it? If you feel you would be distracted from a special television program you wish to watch, you can simply choose not to work that evening.

Youthful baby-sitters are difficult to get these days, and many parents prefer older people. I have even known pleasant and interesting friendships to develop with parents, regardless of age difference. They usually appreciate your need for comfort and do not object to your making a cup of coffee. They may even pick you up and drive you home.

Working mothers with young children are in greater numbers than ever. In some cases sitters are needed for an entire day; other cases call for them to be available after school hours. The daytime hours may appeal to you more than sitting at night, and you may be able to work out a regular schedule.

Getting started requires only a small cash investment, such as placing a small advertisement in the Yellow Pages of the telephone book or in the classified section of your local newspaper. You can mail a circular to every home in the area or distribute them yourself. Be prepared to give references as to your reliability, your health, and your temperament.

Handyman. In these times, if you are a handyman you are very lucky. It is a trade in great demand, and provides a ready-made opportunity for going into a

business of your own. A fix-it business has excellent
chances of succeeding—every home is filled with appli-
ances and gadgets. Repair work is always being sought
for objects in wood, metal, and china. The more materials you can work with, the more calls you will have.

You will need to set aside a work space and you
may need to invest in some tools and equipment, but
you probably won't need to advertise. A few satisfied
customers will flood you with work.

The Franchise Route

Franchising has become a fantastic business, not only
in this country but worldwide. For many people it offers an excellent way to start their own business.

We must realize that any business can fail, and
many do. However, with franchising, while success
mainly depends on you personally, your success is also
in the interest of the corporation that offers the franchise. The company will cooperate in every way to help
you succeed.

It goes without saying that you should not sign
any contract without having an attorney check it thoroughly. It may be advisable also to have an accountant
check the financial structure.

Obtaining a franchise is a venture that requires
the investment of money as well as careful investigation and study. Here are some publications to help you:

*Small Marketers Aids No. 115. Are You Ready
for Franchising?* Write to the nearest field office of the
Small Business Administration for a free copy.

*Tips on Considering a Franchise. Publication No.
298-A 10373.* To obtain a free copy, write to Council

of Better Business Bureaus, Inc., 1150 17th Street, N.W., Washington, D.C. 20036. Be sure to enclose a self-addressed, stamped, long envelope.

How to Get Started in Your Own Franchised Business, by David D. Seltz. You can secure a copy of this book by sending a check or money order for $10 to Farnsworth Publishing Company, 381 Sunrise Highway, Lynbrook, New York 11563, or directly to the author at 240 Madison Avenue, New York, N.Y. 10016.

Owning Your Own Business, by David D. Seltz. This cassette was listed earlier. It is equally useful in a franchise business.

Here is a list of paperbacks published by Pilot Books, Inc., 347 Fifth Avenue, New York, N.Y. 10016:

> *Financial Security & Independence Through a Small Business Franchise* ($2).
>
> *Franchise Investigation and Contract Negotiation* ($2).
>
> *A Woman's Guide to Her Own Franchised Business* ($2).
>
> *Pilot's Question and Answer Guide to Successful Franchising* ($1).
>
> *Directory of Franchising Organizations,* revised annually ($2.50).

WORKING FOR THE GOVERNMENT

Some of the jobs discussed in this section are not actually government jobs but are financed through government grants. They pay either a salary or expenses. Some are part-time, others are full-time jobs. Some government programs, especially pilot and demonstration projects, may have a short life. Before you make a decision, write for information to be sure that the program is still in existence and still functioning as it was when this book was written. There may be new programs you'll want to learn about too.

Census Surveys

The Commerce Department's Bureau of the Census maintains a crew of 1,200 to 1,500 part-time interviewers on its payroll, and older people who can qualify are eligible. The physical demands are considerable, and interviewers must be able to drive a car and read a map. For full information, write to Bureau of the Census, U.S. Department of Commerce, in one of the following cities nearest you:

THE NORTHEAST

441 Stuart Street
Boston, Mass. 02116

26 Federal Plaza
New York, N.Y. 10007

21 South Fifth Street
Philadelphia, Pa. 19106

THE WEST

Denver Federal Center
Denver, Colo. 80225

11000 Wilshire Boulevard
W. Los Angeles, Calif. 90024

909 First Avenue
Seattle, Wash. 98104

THE SOUTHEAST

1401 Peachtree Road, N.E.
Atlanta, Ga. 30309

Addison Building
Charlotte, N.C. 28230

THE MIDWEST

536 South Clark Street
Chicago, Ill. 60605

1100 Commerce Street
Dallas, Texas 75202

2100 W. Washington
    Boulevard
Detroit, Mich. 48226

316 North Robert Street
St. Paul, Minn. 55101

Federal Civil Service Jobs

Generally speaking, there are no upper age limits to employment in the federal civil service. Persons under 70 can qualify for regular appointments, and persons over 70 can be given temporary, renewable appointments. For information about the qualifications and examinations, kinds of work, and pay scales, write to U.S. Civil Service Commission, 1900 E Street, N.W., Washington, D.C. 20415.

Foster Grandparent Program

The Administration on Aging funds the Foster Grandparent Program under which low-income persons, age 60 or over, are employed to give love and attention to institutionalized and other needy children. They work about 20 hours a week and are paid at least the federal minimum wage. They receive payment during orientation and in-service training, and are given a transportation allowance. In most work situations they are also provided with uniforms and a daily meal. Further information and the address of the nearest project can be obtained from ACTION, Foster Grandparent Program, 806 Connecticut Avenue, N.W., Washington, D.C. 20525.*

Green Thumb and Green Light Programs

Sponsored by the National Farmer's Union under a grant from the U.S. Department of Labor, these programs provide limited employment to low-income men and women, age 55 or older, in rural areas.

* For faster receipt of a pamphlet with detailed information on the Foster Grandparent Program, as well as for the Peace Corps and VISTA, phone toll-free 800-424-8580.

In the *Green Thumb* program, retired farmers or those persons with a rural background are employed three days a week (for an eight-hour day) to repair or beautify public areas. They are paid at least the present federal minimum wage. The program is now operating in 15 states: Arkansas, Indiana, Kentucky, Minnesota, Nebraska, New Jersey, New York, North Dakota, Oklahoma, Oregon, Pennsylvania, South Dakota, Utah, Virginia, and Wisconsin.

Green Light, an employment program for women, is in operation in rural areas of Arkansas, Indiana, Kentucky, Minnesota, New Jersey, New York, Oklahoma, Pennsylvania, South Dakota, Virginia, and Wisconsin. At wages comparable to those of Green Thumb workers, Green Light employees serve as aides in community service agencies and, through special outreach projects, help to make such services available to the handicapped, the sick, the elderly, and shut-ins.

Information on Green Thumb or Green Light may be obtained from U.S. Department of Labor, 14th Street and Constitution Avenue, N.W., Washington, D.C. 20210.

International Executive Service Corps

This group, similar to SCORE, is made up of retired executives and former owners of small businesses who provide counsel to enterprises in developing countries throughout the world. (SCORE provides such service only in this country, whereas IESC provides service only abroad.) Volunteers for IESC are paid traveling and living expenses. For further information, write to International Executive Service Corps, 545 Madison Avenue, New York, N.Y. 10022.

Peace Corps

With no upper-age-limit policy, the Peace Corps actively recruits people of all ages, including older people, for overseas volunteer service. After a training period in the United States, volunteers are sent to foreign countries to assist in their development in education, agriculture, health, housing, public works, and community programs.

Volunteers receive a living allowance comparable to the wages earned by similarly employed citizens of the host country. Medical care is provided and travel expenses are paid. Vacations are arranged for, and a special allowance is provided for them. A readjustment allowance of $75 per month is set aside for payment at the end of the minimum two-year assignment. Applications may be obtained at all local post offices. For further information write to ACTION, Peace Corps, 806 Connecticut Avenue, N.W., Washington, D.C. 20525.

Senior Aides

This is a limited employment program for low-income men and women, administered by the National Council of Senior Citizens and funded by the Department of Labor. In this pilot project, people of 55 or older work 20 hours a week and are paid at least the federal minimum wage. Most average $2 an hour. The program serves 21 communities, most of which are central urban areas. Aides work in community service agencies in a wide variety of jobs, from child care and adult education to the home health and homemaker services.

For further information write to U.S. Department of Labor, 14th Street and Constitution Avenue, N.W., Washington, D.C. 20210.

Senior Community Service Project

This is also a demonstration project, similar to Senior Aides. It is funded by the Department of Labor and administered by the National Council on the Aging. In it, low-income men and women, 55 or older, work in both urban and rural areas performing a variety of community services. These aides work in Social Security offices, in public housing, and in the food and nutrition programs of the Department of Agriculture. Additional information can be obtained from the U.S. Department of Labor, 14th Street and Constitution Avenue, N.W., Washington, D.C. 20210.

Teacher Corps

Composed of experienced teachers, the Corps provides team leaders for groups of college graduates and undergraduates. Its objective is to expand and improve the educational opportunities of disadvantaged children and to encourage colleges and universities to strengthen their programs of teacher training. Teacher Corps teams are placed in schools in urban slums and rural poverty areas. Work in classrooms is combined with in-service training and participation in community activities. The team leaders are paid wages (comparable to the local scale) by the local school system.

For additional information, see your local school superintendent or write to The Teacher Corps, Office of Education, Department of Health, Education and

Welfare, 400 Maryland Avenue, S.W., Washington, D.C. 20202.

Teachers and Teachers' Aides
(Adult Basic Education)

Teachers and teachers' aides are used in this program to help undereducated persons 16 years of age or older to reach an eighth-grade equivalency. Local public school systems, community colleges, and other agencies conduct these programs. For further information consult the director of adult education in your state education department. He will refer you to the appropriate local program.

Vista

Volunteers in Service to America offers opportunities for volunteers of all ages, with particular talents and experience, to work in impoverished urban and rural areas of the United States. They live with the poor and help them with their daily problems.

VISTA provides in-service training, medical care, and travel and living allowances sufficient for the community where the volunteer works. In addition, a readjustment allowance of $50 a month is set aside for payment at the end of the minimum one-year service. For further information write to ACTION, Volunteers in Service to America, 806 Connecticut Avenue, N.W., Washington, D.C. 20525.

Park Volunteers

This is a new and unusual job opportunity for those who are qualified to render service to the government and to the people who visit the national parks. It offers jobs to professionals, senior citizens, housewives, students, and even youngsters.

Volunteers for this work must be in good health and physically able to carry out their duties. The superintendent of the park where they want to work may ask them to obtain a medical examination, which is paid for by the government.

Volunteers in parks do not receive a salary, but expenses are paid for lodging, meals, local transportation within the area, and any required uniforms. These expenses are also paid during any training period a job may require. Volunteers serve as:

Living history interpreters and guides. Dressed in period costumes, they interpret by example and dialogue the way people lived in different periods of history. The goal is to bring history to life by making the words, actions, and emotions of our ancestors real and meaningful.

Arts and crafts demonstrators. These volunteers demonstrate a skill, such as glassblowing, candlemaking, weaving, or ironworking. Or they may work with children in a simple arts and crafts program.

History, archaeology, and natural science aides. Working with the National Park Service staff in these areas, aides assist in the search for answers, information, and concepts to augment man's storehouse of knowledge and understanding.

Environmental study area assistants. These volunteers work with children and adults in special areas that tell nature's story. The goal is to expose children and adults to more than a textbook explanation of nature and to offer them an opportunity to experience their own involvement with the environment.

Deputy park rangers. These positions are for specially qualified adults only. Deputy park rangers serve as wildlife managers and law enforcers. Those in wildlife management must be highly skilled in the use of firearms and must be able to identify animals. They must have passed the National Rifle Association's hunter safety test or its equivalent. To qualify for the law enforcement program, you must have at least 600 hours of professional law enforcement training or equivalent experience.

To apply for volunteer work in the parks, get Standard Form 170 (application for federal employment) from your post office. In filling it out, be sure to indicate any interests or skills you want to use or develop. If not enough space is provided, mention them in a covering letter.

If you do not know how to answer some of the questions on the form, a post office employee may help you. Explain that you are applying for a volunteer job that pays no salary but does pay expenses. (For your own convenience you might take this book with you for consultation.)

Do not send a letter or the completed Standard Form 170 to Washington, D.C. Mail one or both to the superintendent of the park in which you wish to serve: Superintendent, Name of Park, P.O. Box or Street Address (if listed), City, State, and Zip Code. (See Appendix D.)

Weather Observers (Cooperative)

Permanent residents in a community who have an interest in observing weather may apply to the Weather Bureau to serve as paid or volunteer cooperative weather observers. Age is not stressed, but observers must be able to assume the responsibility of recording official observations. Additional information may be obtained from the U.S. Department of Commerce, National Oceanic and Atmospheric Administration, Environmental Data Service, National Climatic Center, Asheville, North Carolina 28801.

VOLUNTEER WORK

The need for volunteer help varies from place to place. Some communities may encourage volunteers in a certain job, others may not want to use them at all in that same job. Your local chamber of commerce is an excellent source of information about opportunities for volunteer work. So is the League of Women Voters. Also, service organizations, such as the Kiwanis, Lions, and Rotary clubs, will have suggestions for you.

There are many obvious needs for volunteers, and here is a brief list just to start you thinking.

Civic Affairs
Government offices, museums, libraries, hospitals, schools, the courts, the board of elections, and the like —all need volunteers. Inquire at city hall. Your elected representatives (congressmen and senators) have offices where the public is expected to make its wishes known. Volunteers are always welcome.

Politics
If you are interested in politics, by all means volunteer your services to a political organization. Involvement

in politics, on any level, is a good way to stay active
and meet people.

Shut-ins
Wherever handicapped or ill people are confined—
homes for the aged, hospitals, retirement homes, veterans hospitals—there is a great need for volunteers
for such chores as writing letters, doing errands, reading aloud, feeding patients, taking wheelchair patients
to therapy and laboratories, and assisting with recreational activities.

Religious Institutions
Most religious institutions have active community programs nowadays and depend almost exclusively on
volunteers to run them.

Among the not-so-obvious, less-publicized volunteer jobs are these:

Retired Senior Volunteer Program
RSVP serves hospitals, libraries, schools, and other
community projects. Volunteers may request reim-
bursement for transportation expenses and meals.
Further information can be obtained from ACTION,
Retired Senior Volunteer Program, 806 Connecticut
Avenue, N.W., Washington, D.C. 20525. For faster
receipt of information you may also call, toll-free,
800-424-8580.

Savings Bond Salesman
The Savings Bond Division of the Treasury Department uses volunteers to promote the sale of U.S. sav-

ings bonds. If you are interested in helping the government, write to Coordinator of Volunteer Activities, Savings Bond Division, Department of the Treasury, 15th Street and Pennsylvania Avenue, N.W., Washington, D.C. 20220.

Service Corps of Retired Executives
As noted earlier, SCORE enlists retired men and women executives to advise people in small businesses. Such expert advice may well keep some small business from going under or give another small firm just the help it needs to grow. If you are interested in being a SCORE counselor, inquire at the nearest field office of the Small Business Administration.

Volunteers for
International Technical Assistance
VITA is a private, nonprofit organization through which professionals can help individuals, groups, and organizations that need technical assistance for economic and social development projects in the United States as well as abroad.

The work of the international division is carried on chiefly by correspondence, but when funds are available for travel and living expenses, volunteer consultants undertake brief, on-site assignments overseas.

The domestic division of VITA assists antipoverty projects. VITA-USA emphasizes personal contact between the volunteers and those they are helping. In many cases the volunteer travels to the client for on-the-spot consultation; his stay may last from a few hours to several weeks. Travel expenses are paid by VITA.

In addition to a national consulting service, VITA
has local offices in Boston, Houston, Los Angeles, San
Francisco, and Washington, D.C. For more detailed
information and an application form, write to Volunteers for International Technical Assistance, Inc., College Campus, Schenectady, N.Y. 12308.

Consumer Groups
Many communities have volunteer organizations to
deal with all sorts of consumer problems and com-
plaints. To get information on such activities in your
area, inquire at city hall or one of the local service
organizations.

Environmental Protection
A number of groups welcome the services of volunteers in this relatively new activity. The Yellow Pages
of your telephone directory list some groups you may
want to contact. Also, the National Audubon Society
is one organization that uses volunteers in such programs. Either contact your local branch or write to
National Audubon Society, 950 Third Avenue, New
York, N.Y. 10022, for detailed information. The Sierra
Club is another. Either look in your directory for a
local branch or write to National Sierra Club, 220
Bush Street, San Francisco, Calif. 94104, for detailed
information.

SOCIAL SECURITY AND A JOB

There is a local office of the Social Security Administration accessible to every community. If you are earn-

ing money while collecting benefits, the calculations on whether you will lose or gain in the long run can be very involved. When considering taking a job, you should go directly to a Social Security office and discuss the details and any problems or questions you may have. The following discussion just offers some general guidelines.

The amount you are allowed to earn (without penalty) has been increased recently and may be increased again. There is also the chance that you can earn more in some jobs than the Social Security benefits you receive.

When you are working at a job, whether in government or in private industry, you have to pay Social Security taxes on your earnings without regard to retirement status, age, or whether you are receiving benefits under the system. Permanent employees of the government contribute to a special pension fund. However, if your earnings are high enough to raise your average income, your benefits will be increased when you stop working.

If you wish to continue to work and still collect your full benefits, your earned income must not exceed $2,400 annually ($200 per month). On earnings above $200 in any one month, you will lose $1 in benefits for every $2 above this figure.

If you continue to work beyond age 65, your benefits will be increased by one percent each year, even if you do not earn enough to raise your average income. This is called "delayed retirement credit," and it applies to people who continue to work between ages 65 and 72 and who do not collect benefits during this period.

If husband and wife both qualify for Social Security benefits, both can work past 65 and earn up to $2,400 each without losing benefits. To do this, however, they must file for Social Security benefits separately.

TAX DEDUCTIONS

Expenses incurred when you are in business for yourself are tax-deductible, provided they are necessary for the proper operation of such a venture.

Home operation. The mortgage interest, taxes, and depreciation are prorated according to the space being used for the business. The electricity, telephone, and similar items are also prorated in the same way.

Apartment operation. Rent and utilities are prorated according to the use of the space needed.

Office or warehouse operation. You may deduct the full amount of the rent and all utilities.

The following is a list of other deductions that apply to all places of business, whether a home, apartment, or warehouse:

Licenses and permits required by city, county, or state.

Expenses incurred in starting a business.

All city, county, state, and federal taxes paid on a business.

Rental of equipment and automobile.

Depreciation on equipment, furniture, and fixtures, if purchased outright.

Advertising, printing, and sales promotion.

Maintenance of equipment and office supplies.

Prorated mileage, insurance, and maintenance of automobile that is required for the operation of the business.

Note: The Internal Revenue Service requires proof of all deductions on your income tax return, so be sure to keep all bills, canceled checks, or other proof of payment for several years.

It is certainly to your advantage to engage the services of an accountant. Occasionally someone starting a new business is able to find an accountant who will agree to a reduced fee. In any case the fee is tax-deductible, and may prove to be your best investment.

Appendix A

STATE CAPITAL OFFICES
OF THE 50 STATES

FOR TOURIST INFORMATION, including maps, address
the Division of Tourism of the state. For other kinds
of information, write to the specific department or
division that concerns you.

ALABAMA
Montgomery—36104

ALASKA
Juneau—99801

ARIZONA
Phoenix—85007

ARKANSAS
Little Rock—72201

CALIFORNIA
Sacramento—95814

COLORADO
Denver—80203

CONNECTICUT
Hartford—06115

DELAWARE
Dover—19901

FLORIDA
Tallahassee—32304

GEORGIA
Atlanta—30334

HAWAII
Honolulu—96813

IDAHO
Boise—83702

ILLINOIS
Springfield—62706

INDIANA
Indianapolis—46204

IOWA
Des Moines—50319

KANSAS
Topeka—66612

KENTUCKY
Frankfort—40601

LOUISIANA
Baton Rouge—70804

MAINE
Augusta—04330

MARYLAND
Annapolis—21404

MASSACHUSETTS
Boston—02133

MICHIGAN
Lansing—48933

MINNESOTA
St. Paul—55103

MISSISSIPPI
Jackson—39203

MISSOURI
Jefferson City—65101

MONTANA
Helena—59601

NEBRASKA
Lincoln—68509

NEVADA
Carson City—89701

NEW HAMPSHIRE
Concord—03301

NEW JERSEY
Trenton—08625

NEW MEXICO
Santa Fe—87501

NEW YORK
Albany—12224

NORTH CAROLINA
Raleigh—27601

NORTH DAKOTA
Bismarck—58501

OHIO
Columbus—43215

OKLAHOMA
Oklahoma City—73105

OREGON
Salem—97310

PENNSYLVANIA
Harrisburg—17101

RHODE ISLAND
Providence—02903

SOUTH CAROLINA
Columbia—29201

SOUTH DAKOTA
Pierre—57501

TENNESSEE
Nashville—37219

TEXAS
Austin—78711

UTAH
Salt Lake City—84111

VERMONT
Montpelier—05602

VIRGINIA
Richmond—23219

WASHINGTON
Olympia—98504

WEST VIRGINIA
Charleston—25305

WISCONSIN
Madison—53702

WYOMING
Cheyenne—82001

Appendix B

FIELD OFFICE LOCATIONS OF THE SMALL BUSINESS ADMINISTRATION

ALABAMA
908 South 20th Street
Birmingham, Ala. 32505

ALASKA
1016 West 6th Avenue
Anchorage, Alaska 99501

503 Third Avenue
Fairbanks, Alaska 99701

Federal Building
Juneau, Alaska 99801

ARIZONA
122 North Central Avenue
Phoenix, Ariz. 85004

155 East Alameda Street
Tucson, Ariz. 85701

ARKANSAS
600 West Capitol Avenue
Little Rock, Ark. 72201

CALIFORNIA
1130 O Street
Fresno, Calif. 93721

849 South Broadway
Los Angeles, Calif. 90014

532 North Mountain Avenue
San Bernardino, Calif. 92401

110 West C Street
San Diego, Calif. 92101

450 Golden Gate Avenue
San Francisco, Calif. 94102

COLORADO
721 19th Street
Denver, Colo. 80202

CONNECTICUT
450 Maine Street
Hartford, Conn. 06103

DELAWARE
901 Market Street
Wilmington, Del. 19801

FLORIDA
2220 Ponce de Leon
 Boulevard
Coral Gables, Fla. 33134

400 West Bay Street
Jacksonville, Fla. 32202

1803 West Shore Boulevard
Tampa, Fla. 33607

GEORGIA
1401 Peachtree Street, N.E.
Atlanta, Ga. 30309

GUAM
Ada Plaza Center Building
Agana, Guam 96910

HAWAII
1149 Bethel Street
Honolulu, Hawaii 96813

IDAHO
216 North 8th Street
Boise, Idaho 83701

ILLINOIS
219 South Dearborn Street
Chicago, Ill. 60604

502 Monroe Street
Springfield, Ill. 62701

INDIANA
36 South Pennsylvania Street
Indianapolis, Ind. 46204

IOWA
210 Walnut Street
Des Moines, Iowa 50309

KANSAS
120 South Market Street
Wichita, Kans. 67202

KENTUCKY
600 Federal Place
Louisville, Ky. 40202

LOUISIANA
124 Camp Street
New Orleans, La. 70130

MAINE
40 Western Avenue
Augusta, Maine 04330

MARYLAND
Hopkins Plaza
Baltimore, Md. 21201

MASSACHUSETTS
John Fitzgerald Kennedy
   Federal Building
Boston, Mass. 02203

326 Appleton Street
Holyoke, Mass. 01040

MICHIGAN
1249 Washington Boulevard
Detroit, Mich. 48226

201 McClellan Street
Marquette, Mich. 49855

MINNESOTA
12 South 6th Street
Minneapolis, Minn. 55402

MISSISSIPPI
2500 14th Street
Gulfport, Miss. 39501

245 East Capitol Street
Jackson, Miss. 39205

MISSOURI
911 Walnut Street
Kansas City, Mo. 64106

210 North 12th Street
St. Louis, Mo. 63101

MONTANA
Main & 6th Avenue
Helena, Mont. 59601

NEBRASKA
215 North 17th Street
Omaha, Neb. 68102

NEVADA
300 Las Vegas Boulevard
    South
Las Vegas, Nev. 89101

NEW HAMPSHIRE
55 Pleasant Street
Concord, N. H. 03301

NEW JERSEY
970 Broad Street
Newark, N. J. 07102

NEW MEXICO
500 Gold Avenue, S.W.
Albuquerque, N.M. 87101

1015 El Paso Road
Las Cruces, N.M. 88001

NEW YORK
91 State Street
Albany, N.Y. 12297

121 Ellicott Street
Buffalo, N.Y. 14203

26 Federal Plaza
New York, N.Y. 10007

55 St. Paul Street
Rochester, N.Y. 14604

Fayette & Salina Streets
Syracuse, N.Y. 13202

NORTH CAROLINA
222 South Church Street
Charlotte, N.C. 28202

NORTH DAKOTA
653 2nd Avenue, North
Fargo, N.D. 58102

OHIO
550 Main Street
Cincinnati, Ohio 45202

1240 East 9th Street
Cleveland, Ohio 44199

50 West Gay Street
Columbus, Ohio 43215

OKLAHOMA
30 North Hudson Street
Oklahoma City, Okla. 73102

OREGON
921 S.W. Washington Street
Portland, Ore. 97205

PENNSYLVANIA
(Philadelphia area)
1 Decker Square
Bala Cynwyd, Pa. 19004

1000 Liberty Avenue
Pittsburgh, Pa. 15222

PUERTO RICO
255 Ponce de Leon Avenue
Hato Rey, Puerto Rico 00919

RHODE ISLAND
57 Eddy Street
Providence, R.I. 02903

SOUTH CAROLINA
1801 Assembly Street
Columbia, S.C. 29201

SOUTH DAKOTA
8th & Main Avenue
Sioux Falls, S.D. 57102

TENNESSEE
502 South Gay Street
Knoxville, Tenn. 37902

167 North Main Street
Memphis, Tenn. 38103

500 Union Street
Nashville, Tenn. 37219

TEXAS
701 North Upper Broadway
Corpus Christi, Texas 78401

1100 Commerce Street
Dallas, Texas 75202

109 North Oregon Street
El Paso, Texas 79901

219 East Jackson Street
Harlingen, Texas 78550

808 Travis Street
Houston, Texas 77002

1205 Texas Avenue
Lubbock, Texas 79408

505 East Travis Street
Marshall, Texas 75670

301 Broadway
San Antonio, Texas 78205

UTAH
125 South State Street
Salt Lake City, Utah 84111

VERMONT
87 State Street
Montpelier, Vt. 05601

VIRGINIA
400 North 8th Street
Richmond, Va. 23240

WASHINGTON
710 Second Avenue
Seattle, Wash. 98104

Courthouse Building
Spokane, Wash. 99210

WASHINGTON, D.C.
1310 L Street, N.W.
Washington, D.C. 20417

WEST VIRGINIA
500 Quarrier Street
Charleston, W.Va. 25301

109 North Third Street
Clarksburg, W.Va. 26301

WISCONSIN
520 South Barstow Street
Eau Claire, Wis. 54701

25 West Main Street
Madison, Wis. 53703

735 West Wisconsin Avenue
Milwaukee, Wis. 53203

WYOMING
300 North Center Street
Casper, Wyo. 82601

Appendix C

ORGANIZATIONS OF
INTEREST TO RETIREES
AND FUTURE RETIREES

THE ADVANTAGES of being a member of the three non-profit, nonpartisan organizations given below are so numerous that I will not attempt to list them. You can write to the organizations for complete information and then judge for yourself.

I am a member of all three (though not connected in any official capacity), and I have been so favorably impressed with them that I suggest you join all three. Membership in each is open to both men and women. Each has low-cost annual dues.

American Association of Retired Persons
1909 K Street, N.W.
Washington, D.C. 20006

Membership is open to those 55 years of age or over, whether retired or not. Dues: $2 per year, or $5 for three years, which includes a subscription to its bi-monthly magazine *Modern Maturity* and to its monthly *AARP News Bulletin*. This association has a special division called Action for Independent Maturity (AIM), which is open to men and women 50 to 65 years of age who are still working. AIM prepares its members for retirement through educational materials on the subject. Dues: $3 per year, which includes a subscription to its bimonthly magazine *Dynamic Maturity*. Membership in one or the other includes spouse.

National Council of Senior Citizens, Inc.
1511 K Street, N.W.
Washington, D.C. 20005

Membership is open to those of any age, retired or not. The dues are $4 per year which includes subscription to its monthly publication *Senior Citizens News*. Spouse membership fee is only $1 extra per year.

Senior Advocates International, Inc.
1825 K Street, N.W.
Washington, D.C. 20006

Membership is open to those 50 years of age and over, retired or not. They also welcome anyone who supports the needs and interests of people over 50. Dues, which includes subscription to its bimonthly magazine *Senior Advocate,* are $5 for one year or $13 for three years. Membership includes spouse.

Appendix D

ADDRESSES OF
THE NATIONAL PARKS

FOR COMPLETE tourist information, address your letter to the superintendent of the particular park that interests you. You can also write to the national office for general information. Its address is:

National Park Service
1100 L Street, N.W.
Washington, D.C. 20005

At this writing, all the parks listed below, with the exception of Canyonlands National Park and North Cascades National Park, offer jobs under the Volunteers in Parks program.

There are many state parks in addition to the national parks. Write to the Division of Tourism at the state capital offices of the state you plan to visit. (See Appendix A.) The Volunteers in Parks program is conducted only at national parks.

Acadia National Park
P.O. Box 338
Bar Harbor, Maine 04609

Big Bend National Park
Texas 79834

Bryce Canyon National Park
Bryce Canyon, Utah 84717

Canyonlands National Park
Post Office Building
Moab, Utah 84532

Carlsbad Caverns Nat'l Park
P.O. Box 1598
Carlsbad, N. Mex. 88220

Crater Lake Nat'l Park
P.O. Box 7
Crater Lake, Ore. 97604

Everglades National Park
P.O. Box 279
Homestead, Fla. 33030

Glacier National Park
West Glacier, Mont. 59936

Grand Canyon Nat'l Park
P.O. Box 129
Grand Canyon, Ariz. 86023

Grand Teton National Park
P.O. Box 67
Moose, Wyo. 83012

Great Smoky Mountains
    National Park
Gatlinburg, Tenn. 37738

Haleakala National Park
P.O. Box 456
Kahului, Maui
Hawaii 96732

Hawaii Volcanoes
    National Park
Hawaii 96718

Hot Springs National Park
Box 1219
Ark. 71901

Isle Royale National Park
87 North Ripley Street
Houghton, Mich. 49931

Kings Canyon Nat'l Park
(See Sequoia and Kings
    Canyon National Parks.)

Lassen Volcanic National
    Park
Mineral, Calif. 96063

Mammoth Cave Nat'l Park
Mammoth Cave
Ky. 42259

Mesa Verde National Park
Colo. 81330

Mt. McKinley Nat'l Park
McKinley Park
Alaska 99755

Mt. Ranier National Park
Longmire, Wash. 98397

North Cascades National
    Park
Sedro Woolley, Wash. 98284

Olympic National Park
600 East Park Avenue
Port Angeles, Wash. 98362

Petrified Forest National
    Park
Box 518
Holbrook, Ariz. 86025

Platt National Park
P.O. Box 201
Sulphur, Okla. 73086

Rocky Mountain National
    Park
P.O. Box 1080
Estes Park, Colo. 80517

Sequoia and Kings Canyon
    National Parks
Three Rivers, Calif. 93217

Shenandoah Nat'l Park
Luray, Va. 22835

Virgin Islands Nat'l Park
P.O. Box 1717
Charlotte Amalie
St. Thomas, V.I. 00801

Wind Cave National Park
Hot Springs, S. Dak. 57747

Yellowstone National Park
Wyo. 82190

Yosemite National Park
P.O. Box 577
Calif. 95389

Zion National Park
Springdale, Utah 84767

Appendix E

MOTELS YOU CAN AFFORD

HERE are the headquarters addresses of eight motel chains whose rates are modest. Write to them for a copy of their directories listing all locations, facilities, and rates.

American Family Lodge
470 South Colorado
   Boulevard
Denver, Colo. 80222

Chalet Susse International, Inc.
2 Progress Avenue
Nashua, N.H. 03060

Days Inns of America, Inc.
2751 Buford Highway, N.E.
Atlanta, Ga. 30324

Econo-Travel Motor Hotel Corp.
Three Koger Executive
   Center
Norfolk, Va. 23502

Imperial 400 Motels
375 Sylvan Avenue
Englewood Cliffs, N.J. 07632

Motel 6 Administrative Office
P.O. Box 3550
Santa Barbara, Calif. 93105

Regal 8 Inns, Executive Offices
P.O. Box 1268
Mt. Vernon, Ill. 62864

Scottish Inns of America, Inc.
Executive Offices
125 North Kentucky Street
Kingston, Tenn. 37763

Recently 145 colleges in the United States and Canada have made their recreational and cultural facilities available to the general public. Their fees are a fraction of commercial prices. For a copy of *Guide to Low-Cost Vacations and Lodgings on College Campuses,* write to CMG Publications, Box 630, Princeton, N.J. 08540. The price is $4.50.

Appendix F

MEXICO: WHAT YOU SHOULD DO BEFORE CROSSING THE BORDER

AUTOMOBILE INSURANCE

If you want to drive your car into Mexico, even for just a short sightseeing trip across the border, be sure to obtain automobile insurance issued by a Mexican insurance company. Automobile insurance issued by a company in any other country is not valid in Mexico.

In the event of an accident, a motorist (guilty or not) and his car are usually detained until full payment of the damage or claim has been made *in cash*.

Mexican automobile insurance is available for short visits or stays. The rate is about $2 to $3 per day. (The insurance rates are set by the Mexican government.) I recommend that you buy your insurance from Sanborn's Mexican Insurance Service. Write to Sanborn's, P.O. Box 1210, McAllen, Texas 78501, for a free copy of *Sanborn's Mexico Travel-Aid and Trip-Planner,* which explains their services. Each Sanborn agency is a licensed, authorized agent for Mexico's largest insurance companies. Insurance bought at any of them costs no more than when purchased through any other agency.

When you pay a premium of more than $7.50 but do not stay in Mexico as long as you had planned, the unused portion of your policy will be refunded (less the $7.50) when you leave Mexico. Only Sanborn's has refunding offices at all major gateways.

Also ask about their Travelog service. If you purchase your Mexican automobile insurance at one of their offices, they will give you a free, mile-by-mile "Travelog" based on your itinerary. These Travelogs show the latest road directions in detail and are filled with practical travel tips and suggestions on driving in Mexico. The restaurants and rooms they recommend have been personally inspected by Mr. Sanborn.

Here are the locations of Sanborn's Mexican Insurance Service offices along the border:

Arizona:	Douglas, Lukeville, Nogales, Yuma
California:	El Centro, San Ysidro
New Mexico:	Deming
Texas:	Brownsville, Del Rio, Eagle Pass, El Paso, Laredo, McAllen, Presidio, Roma

TOURIST CARD

If you are going to stay more than 72 hours at the border area, or if you are going farther into Mexico, you must have a Mexican Tourist Card, which is good for six months and can then be renewed. Your car, however, is limited to a stay of 180 days, although the Mexican government will allow for special circumstances such as illness or accident.

The Tourist Card can be obtained at any of the Mexican Immigration Offices, which are located in the Mexican cities along the border. To qualify for a Tourist Card, each person over the age of 15 must show proof of citizenship (Army or Navy discharge papers, birth certificate, naturalization papers, passport, or voter registration card).

If you, as an American citizen, are en route and do not have any of these with you, Sanborn's can notarize an affidavit for you that will be accepted by the Mexican immigration officials.

PETS

To take your dog or cat into Mexico, you must have with you a veterinarian's certificate showing that your pet has been given anti-rabies shots within the last six months. If shots have not been given, kennels in U.S. border towns will take care of them.

Appendix G

MOBILE HOMES AND
MOBILE HOME PARKS

MORE THAN 7 MILLION Americans live in mobile homes. The purchase of mobile homes in 1973 exceeded all records: More than 600,000 were sold.

They make great sense for retirees, because they provide an economical, easy way of living. They allow retirees to settle down for a trial period in a certain area or to take a prolonged vacation. You can have a mobile home shipped to any new location you choose.

Investigate the various makes and models by visiting dealers. You will be pleasantly surprised to find that most mobile homes are well equipped and furnished. They are less costly than unfurnished conventional homes, and they are certainly less costly to maintain.

Financing the purchase of a mobile home can easily be arranged through a dealer, through most banks, or through any savings and loan association. It is also possible to rent one. If you have bought a mobile home and later want to give it up, you can either rent it to others or sell it.

Here are some useful publications on mobile homes and mobile home parks:

Tips on Mobile Home Selection. For a free copy of this helpful booklet, send a self-addressed, *long* envelope and 20 cents in stamps to Mobile Home Tips, Dept. CBBB, Box 32, Chantilly, Va. 22021.

Mobile Homes. This 96-page yearbook (in magazine form) contains articles about mobile home living and answers questions on finance, construction, maintenance, and placement. You can obtain a copy by sending a check or money order for $1.25 to Mobile Homes Magazine, Box 32, Chantilly, Va. 22021.

Buying and Financing a Mobile Home (145B). For a free copy of this 12-page government pamphlet, write to Consumer Information, Public Documents Distribution Center, Pueblo, Colo. 81009.

All About Mobile Homes, by John L. Scherer. Everything you need to know about selecting, financing, and selling a mobile home, as well as how to choose a mobile home park. To obtain a copy, send a check or money order for 95 cents (plus 15 cents to cover mailing and handling) to Mail Order Department, Fawcett Publications, Greenwich, Conn. 06830.

Woodall's Mobile Home and Park Directory. This directory lists the facilities and rates of more than 13,000 national mobile home parks and communities that were visited, inspected, and rated by Woodall's 80 field representatives. In addition, it contains a special Buyers' Guide on Mobile Homes. To secure a copy, send a check or money order for $5.95 (plus 55 cents for postage and handling) to Woodall Publishing Company, 500 Hyacinth Place, Highland Park, Ill. 60035.

Florida Mobile Home Guide. For those interested in locating in Florida, this special guide contains an exclusive list of Florida's mobile home parks, mobile home subdivisions, and their rates and facilities. To

obtain a copy, send a check or money order for $2 to
Mobile Home News, Inc., P.O. Box 967, Kendall
Branch, Miami, Fla. 33156.

Mobile Home Manual. This is a complete mobile
home encyclopedia in two volumes, fully indexed for
quick reference. Its thousands of photos, drawings,
diagrams, useful facts, and professional tips will save
you time and money. It costs $9 plus 35 cents to cover
postage and handling and is published by Trail-R-Club
of America, Box 1376, Beverly Hills, Calif. 90213.

Appendix H

RECREATIONAL VEHICLES
(CAMPERS, MOTOR HOMES,
AND TRAVEL TRAILERS)

RECREATIONAL VEHICLES are giving millions of people a low-cost way to camp, vacation, or travel. They offer an additional opportunity to retirees, who can sell their furniture, give it away, or put it in storage for possible use at some future time and go to live in a warm-climate area during the winter and a cool one during the summer.

Last but not least, a camper, motor home, or travel trailer offers a real vacation for your wife, because it is so much easier to take care of than an apartment or house.

A recreational vehicle means you can travel at low cost. It not only provides transportation but also serves as your hotel. As an additional convenience, you will not have any packing and unpacking to do. If your furnishings include a stove, you can have home-cooked meals. Indeed, you can go anywhere—stop when you want, go when you have the urge—and have your home right there with you. It gives you a turtle's convenience and protection.

With proper care, a camper, motor home, or travel trailer will last for many money-saving years. When it isn't in use, and if it can be parked near your residence, it can serve as an extra bedroom for guests.

Or it can be rented to others to provide extra income, while at the same time you may get a tax-deduction allowance.

Naturally, there is some difference between driving a standard passenger car and driving a recreational vehicle. Most good drivers should not encounter any difficulty learning to handle a camper or motor home. There is, however, a certain knack to hauling a travel trailer. But it may be worth the extra time to learn to drive one, because a travel trailer can be parked. This gives you the independent use of your car.

The fact that there are more than 4 million recreational vehicles in use and being driven by older as well as young people offers sufficient proof that it can be done. But while some people are good drivers of their automobile, they may not, for some reason, be able to handle a camper, motor home, or travel trailer. Those people should leave the driving to others.

There is one point to remember if you are going to use a travel trailer: *Do not allow children or others to ride in it.* They should ride in the passenger car. In some states riding in a trailer is against the law. Even if it isn't, you should be aware that it is dangerous.

The use of recreational vehicles for camping, vacations, and traveling has grown so large that General Motors has entered the field and is now manufacturing motor homes. Ford Motor Company is making a slide-in camper to fit its Super-Camper Special Pickup Truck.

People who would like to own a camper, motor home, or travel trailer but who have some doubts about it should try renting one first.

Trail-R-Club of America (Box 1376, Beverly Hills, Calif. 90213) publishes a number of good books on recreational vehicles. *How to Buy Recreation Vehicles* ($2.95) discusses the pros and cons of trailers, pickup campers, tent trailers, and motor homes. *Recreation Vehicle Buyers Guide* ($3.95) provides a listing of recreational vehicles with full specifications and other information. *Pickup Camper Manual* ($4.95) describes how to buy, operate, modify, and maintain these popular vehicles. Sample topic: How to select the proper truck. *Motor Home Manual* ($4.95) is a veritable encyclopedia on the subject of motor homes. And *Trailer Owner's Manual* ($3.75) is a well-illustrated guidebook for trailer owners.

Before starting on a vacation with a recreational vehicle, it's a good idea to know something about the camping facilities in the vicinity. Here are several camping and park directories you may find useful:

Camping in the National Park System (*249B*). To obtain a copy of this 28-page booklet, write to Consumer Information, Public Documents Distribution Center, Pueblo, Colo. 81009. Include a check or money order for 55¢, payable to the Superintendent of Documents.

Woodall's Trailering Parks & Campgrounds. Send check or money order for $6.95 (plus 55¢ for postage and handling) to Woodall Publishing Company, 500 Hyacinth Place, Highland Park, Ill. 60035. This directory lists all known U.S. parks and campgrounds, giving their location, description, and Woodall's rating of the site. It also contains 64 pages of maps.

Florida Camping and R.V. Guide. Send a check or money order for $2 to Mobile Home News, Inc., P.O. Box 967, Kendall Branch, Miami, Fla. 33156. For those especially interested in Florida, this guide contains a list of the campsites in Florida's state and national parks plus a list of all private campgrounds in the state. Information on rates and facilities is included.

The use of recreational vehicles has become so popular that many large corporations maintain camping and parking areas all over the world, and are now in the process of building more. Still, many more are needed.

The following companies issue directories giving the locations of their campgrounds, the facilities available at each, and their rates. All of the directories are available free of charge.

Crazy Horse Campgrounds
2152 DuPont Drive
Newport Beach, Calif. 92664

Holiday Inns, Inc.
Trav-L-Park Department
Holiday City
Memphis, Tenn. 38118

Jellystone Campgrounds Ltd.
236 Michigan Street
Sturgeon Bay, Wis. 54235

Kampgrounds of America, Inc. (KOA)
P.O. Box 1138
Billings, Mont. 59103

Ramada Camp Inns
P.O. Box 1632
Phoenix, Ariz. 85001

Venture Out in America, Inc.
(A Division of Gulf Oil Corporation)
3445 Peachtree Road, N.E.
Atlanta, Ga. 30326

A free copy of the KOA directory can be picked up at any KOA campground. To obtain a copy by mail, send a $1 check or money order to the address above. Those who write for a copy will receive a special, 120-page "Bonus Edition," which contains $75 worth of coupons good at major tourist attractions across the country.

Suggested Reading

RELOCATION

Safe Places, by David and Holly Franke. Published by Arlington House, 81 Centre Avenue, New Rochelle, N.Y. 10801. $13.95.

This unusual hardcover book lists 47 low-crime-rate cities in 35 states of this country, allowing for a varied choice of climate. Nearly all the cities discussed are small towns. For each city, there is detailed information on the following: the crime rate; renting and purchasing houses, apartments, farms, and ranches in the area; educational and medical facilities; jobs, including part-time work; taxes; climate; pollution levels; population; recreational facilities; shopping and public transportation; utilities; community life; clubs and fraternal organizations.

The book is available in two separate paperback editions called *Safe Places East* and *Safe Places West.* They are published by Warner Paperback Library, 315 Park Avenue South, New York, N.Y. 10010, and are priced at only $1.95 each. The Mississippi River is the geographical divider, with 22 cities east of it and 25 cities west of it. For the 15 states not covered in the two books, the authors list in an appendix where information on safe places in these states can be obtained.

David Franke has also written a book called *America's 50 Safest Cities* (Arlington House, $8.95).

Some retired people may prefer moving to a city, rather than a small town, due to the additional facilities and jobs that most cities offer. This book lists 50 cities, ranging in population from 50,148 to 111,662, that are judged safest in comparison to other cities of population 50,000 or over.

Where to Retire on a Small Income, by Norman D.
    Ford. Published by Harian Publications, Green-
    lawn, N.Y. 11740. $2.50.

Cities, towns, farming areas, and retirement communities in New England, New York, New Jersey, Pennsylvania, Delaware, West Virginia, Maryland, the Atlantic Coast states to Florida, the Gulf states, the Ozark Mountain regions, the Midwest, the Southwest, the Far West—it's all here. And for those who want the benefits of retiring to a tropical climate outside the continental United States but don't want to live in a foreign country, the book recommends Hawaii and the territorial islands of Puerto Rico and the Virgin Islands.

This book offers complete details on climate and contains information on low-priced land, low-priced existing homes and farms, business opportunities, clubs and fraternal organizations, cultural activities, jobs for the retired, libraries, living costs, recreational and shopping facilities, population, scenery, taxes, and transportation.

Harian Publications also publishes books that cover in greater detail conditions in the three states that are most often chosen by retired people:

All About Arizona—The Healthful State, by Thomas
B. Lesure. $2.95.

All About California—The State That Has Everything,
by Thomas B. Lesure. $2.50.

*Norman Ford's Florida—Where to Go for Whatever
You Seek in Florida,* by Norman D. Ford. $3.00.

LIVING IN THE COUNTRY

Buying Country Property, by Herbert R. Moral. Garden Way Publishing Co., Charlotte, Vermont
05445. Special paperback edition, $3.00. This
book is also published in a standard paperback
edition by Bantam Books, 660 Fifth Avenue, New
York, N.Y. 10019 ($1.75).

Some of the chapter titles are: How to Get the
Most Out of Realtors; Facts to Remember About Land;
How to Judge the True Condition of an Old House,
and the 25 Sources of Trouble to Check Before Buying It; When Is It Worthwhile to Remodel, and How
to Remodel; Getting the Most Mortgage for the Least
Money.

Buying Country Property: Pitfalls and Pleasures, by
Irving Price. Published by Harper & Row, 10 E.
53rd Street, New York, N.Y. 10022 ($5.95).
Also available in paperback from Pyramid Publications, 919 Third Avenue, New York, N.Y.
10022 ($1.50).

Included are chapters on mortgage financing, zon-
ing, surveys, sewage systems, and utilities and building
construction.

How to Locate in the Country: Your Personal Guide,
    by John Gourlie. Garden Way Publishing Co.,
    Charlotte, Vermont 05445. Hardcover $4.50,
    paperback $2.50.

Unlike the two books listed above, this book is
not about buying property. The author evaluates different localities and geographical areas to enable you to
select the places most suitable to you. There are maps,
a 21-point checklist, information directories, and com-
mentaries to help you make a decision.

Country Living: A Guide for City People, by Jerome
    Belanger. Published by Universal-Award House,
    Inc., 235 East 45th Street, New York, N.Y. 10017
    ($1.50 plus 25¢ for postage and handling).

The author, who lives on and operates his own
farm in Wisconsin, is the editor and publisher of *Countryside* magazine. Every person who wants to buy a
farm or land or a house in the country should read this
book before making such a purchase. But its usefulness
doesn't end there. Its more than 250 pages are filled
with practical advice and ideas for people who already
live in the country.

Remember the victory gardens of World War II?
Now there are "inflation gardens." This book suggests
ways to make them productive.

FINANCIAL AND CONSUMER INFORMATION

1974 Tax Facts. Published by the American Association of Retired Persons, 1909 K Street, N.W., Washington, D.C. 20006. Free.

This 57-page paperback book describes income taxes, property taxes, sales taxes, and other taxes in all 50 states and the District of Columbia. It will answer your questions about the advantages or disadvantages of one state over another: For example, six states have no income tax, four have no sales tax, and eleven states allow an exemption to their sales tax for certain items such as food. This book also has information on tax exemptions or concessions for people over 60. Some states draw the line at age 62, most at 65, and one at 70. Seven states make no concessions for any age.

The booklet points out that because state laws are subject to change every year, you should write to the state capital for the latest information.

Consumer Protection, Interstate Land Sales. Office of Interstate Land Sales Registration, U.S. Department of Housing and Urban Development, Washington, D.C. 20410. Free.

If you are thinking of buying land through an offer made by developers, where 50 or more parcels are often handled, you should know the facts. The law requires land developers to file a statement regarding the availability of access roads, sewer services, water, utilities, and so on. Even if the developer has filed such a statement, it does not mean that the government has inspected or approved the development or the value, if any, of the property.

If you are contemplating such an investment, be sure to make a personal inspection of the lot or acreage and the surrounding area before you buy. Do not sign any contract without having a lawyer review the property description and the small print.

Don't Be Gypped (063B). Consumer Information, Public Documents Distribution Center, Pueblo, Colo. 81009. Free.

This four-page pamphlet explains bait-and-switch advertising and how to protect yourself against it. If you have been cheated through an advertisement, this pamphlet will tell you how to report it to the Federal Trade Commission.

Consumer Information Index. Consumer Information, Public Documents Distribution Center, Pueblo, Colo. 81009. Free.

This booklet contains a list of government publications related to purchase, use, and care of consumer products as well as many other useful subjects.

MISCELLANEOUS

Changing Times, The Kiplinger Magazine. Available by subscription only. Editors Park, Maryland 20782. Yearly subscription: $7.00.

This monthly publication is not intended for retired people as such. It specializes in ideas and has advice on such subjects as shopping, saving money, health, taxes, automobiles, housing, gardening, pets, vacations, recreation, hobbies, education, jobs, and investing. All new subscribers receive a free copy of *99 New Ideas on Your Money, Job, and Living.*

Retirement Living. Harvest Years Publishing Company, Inc., 150 East 58th Street, New York, N.Y. 10022. Yearly subscription: $6.00.

This monthly magazine features articles by experts in their field, and it contains much useful information. It often includes interesting accounts of personal experiences.

Harvest Years Publishing also publishes "Retirement Living Guides" at $1.25 each. One guide is titled *The Law and Your Retirement;* another, *Money and Your Retirement.* To obtain one or both of these guides, write to the above address care of Harvest Years Publishing Company.

Garden Way Publishing Company (Charlotte, Vermont 05445) puts out a wide range of "how to" books. Each book deals with a special subject. Among them are: growing fruits or vegetables; raising chickens, pigs, beef, or lambs; raising cows or goats for milk; keeping beehives; and taking care of horses. Garden Way's catalog lists these and more than 100 other books on many practical, useful subjects—for example, how to use honey in cooking, how to grow food and flowers in containers all year, and how to use companion plants. (The book on the latter subject contains such helpful tips as keeping rabbits out by planting an onion or garlic border.) A book titled *How to Retire in the Country* is scheduled for publication in November 1974.

Send $1 to Garden Way and request a copy of their catalog. It will be sent to you along with a "Deposit-Refund Certificate" good for $1 toward any order.